Herbert Myrick

Turkeys and How to Grow Them

A treatise on the natural history and origin of the name of turkeys; the various breeds, and best methods to insure success in the business of turkey growing. With essays from practical turkey growers in different parts

Herbert Myrick

Turkeys and How to Grow Them

A treatise on the natural history and origin of the name of turkeys; the various breeds, and best methods to insure success in the business of turkey growing. With essays from practical turkey growers in different parts

ISBN/EAN: 9783337292140

Printed in Europe, USA, Canada, Australia, Japan

Cover: Foto ©Andreas Hilbeck / pixelio.de

More available books at **www.hansebooks.com**

TURKEYS

– AND –

How to Grow Them.

A treatise on the natural history and origin of the Name of Turkeys; the Various Breeds, and Best Methods to insure success in the business of Turkey growing. With Essays from Practical Turkey Growers in different parts of the United States and Canada.

EDITED BY HERBERT MYRICK.

With the assistance of Samuel Cushman, late Poultry Manager Rhode Island Experiment Station; Breeds and Show Points treated by H. S. Babcock, Secretary Rhode Island Poultry Association and Editor American Standard of Perfection; Articles by George Wolf, Judge of Turkeys at Chicago Fat Stock Show, A. F. Greene of Massachusetts, E. Richardson of California, George Enty of Pennsylvania, J. F. Barbee of Kentucky, and other famous breeders of Thoroughbred Turkeys, or specialists in raising Turkeys for market.

COPIOUSLY ILLUSTRATED.

NEW YORK
ORANGE JUDD COMPANY
1899

Copyright, 1897,
BY ORANGE JUDD COMPANY

PREFACE.

No book in existence gives an adequate account of the turkey,—its development from the wild state to the various breeds, and complete directions for breeding, feeding, rearing and marketing these beautiful and profitable birds. The present book is an effort to fill this gap. It is based upon the experience of the most successful experts in turkey growing, both as breeders of fancy stock and as raisers of turkeys for market. In the preparation of the work we make full use of the valuable and original work on turkey culture done at the Rhode Island Experiment Station, quote from Harris' (English) Turkey Book, and print the prize-winning papers out of nearly two hundred essays submitted by the most successful turkey growers in America. We have also given one essay on turkey culture, from different parts of the country, including Canada and New Brunswick, that the reader may see what ways have proven successful in each locality. A method that succeeds in Tennessee might not do in Nebraska; the cold winters of Vermont would kill the turkeys if the systems were in vogue there that succeed in Southern Missouri.

Much of the compilation has been done by Mr. Aaron F. Greene, who includes also many points from his own experience, as well as many points contained in the numerous essays not printed, that will help to success in rearing turkeys for profit and pleasure. It is thus hoped that the book will be found comprehensive and useful and to contain all that is of practical interest on this subject.

EXTENT OF THE TURKEY BUSINESS.

We are also able to present some fairly accurate statistics as to the extent of the poultry industry in the United States. It is probable that the annual sales of turkeys for meat exceed the number of turkeys enumerated by the census of 1890—over 10,000,000. With the sales of breeding stock and eggs, it is probable that the turkey trade of the United States exceeds $12,000,000 annually. The principal turkey-growing States appear in the tables below, and the *American Agriculturist* has shown that the number in the United States June 1, 1896, was over 12,000,000. We also copy a table from that magazine, showing the turkeys in the principal turkey counties of these States, from some of which choice breeding stock is shipped to all parts of this country, England and Europe.

NUMBER OF TURKEYS IN EACH STATE ON JUNE 1, 1890, ACCORDING TO THE FEDERAL CENSUS.

Total for United States, 10,754,060.

State	Number	State	Number
Maine	15,259	Missouri	928,751
New Hampshire	10,207	North Dakota	33,928
Vermont	72,164	South Dakota	60,163
Massachusetts	5,805	Nebraska	218,636
Rhode Island	11,656	Kansas	530,397
Connecticut	30,176	Kentucky	672,106
New York	402,642	Tennessee	430,333
New Jersey	162,270	Alabama	177,681
Pennsylvania	535,828	Mississippi	194,398
Delaware	70,578	Louisiana	74,680
Maryland	278,522	Texas	535,916
District of Columbia	215	Oklahoma	5,931
Virginia	477,414	Arkansas	118,816
West Virginia	214,756	Montana	5,077
North Carolina	197,420	Wyoming	2,441
South Carolina	149,126	Colorado	20,872
Georgia	148,797	New Mexico	928
Florida	34,426	Arizona	2,744
Ohio	521,171	Utah	9,220
Indiana	505,111	Nevada	4,193
Illinois	1,043,947	Idaho	6,433
Michigan	185,847	Washington	17,187
Wisconsin	206,230	Oregon	43,555
Minnesota	151,459	California	287,799
Iowa	940,849	Total	10,754,060

PREFACE. vii

The principal turkey counties, showing the number of turkeys in each in June, 1889, as returned by the census, also the number on Jan 1, 1896, as estimated by *American Agriculturist*, are as follows:

Last three figures (000's) omitted.

	1889	'96		1889	'96
VERMONT.	72	83	Nash	5	5
Addison Co.	12	14	Others	169	179
Orange	13	15	SOUTH CAROLINA	149	156
Windsor	14	16	Abbeville	6	6
Others	33	38	Beaufort	13	14
NEW YORK	403	483	Berkeley	8	8
Erie Co	5	6	Darlington	7	7
Monroe	13	15	Edgefield	7	7
Onondaga	15	18	Others	108	114
St. Lawrence	30	36	GEORGIA	149	164
Steuben	8	9	Bartow	3	3
Others	332	399	Burke	4	4
NEW JERSEY	162	194	Houston	3	3
Burlington Co	26	31	Screven	4	4
Hunterdon	16	18	Thomas	3	3
Mercer	17	20	Others	132	147
Monmouth	22	26	OHIO	521	599
Salem	22	26	Fairfield	8	9
Others	59	73	Franklin	10	11
PENNSYLVANIA	536	589	Montgomery	12	13
Berks	23	24	Preble	9	10
Chester	37	40	Others	482	556
Lancaster Co	30	33	INDIANA	505	581
Washington	31	34	Boone	11	12
York	23	25	Hendricks	15	17
Others	393	433	Henry	13	15
DELAWARE	71	78	Montgomery	13	15
Kent	39	43	Putnam	13	15
Newcastle	12	13	Others	440	507
Sussex	20	22	ILLINOIS	1044	1252
MARYLAND	279	307	Iroquois	30	36
Charles	19	21	Lee	21	25
Frederick	19	21	Livingston	22	26
Harford	16	18	McLean	25	31
Queen Anne	24	26	Vermilion	34	40
St. Mary	21	23	Others	912	1094
Others	180	198	MICHIGAN	186	214
VIRGINIA	477	525	Kent	8	9
Princess Anne	18	20	Lenawee	14	16
Rockingham	21	23	Monroe	7	8
Tazewell	13	14	Oakland	10	12
Washington	14	15	Washtenaw	13	15
Wythe	12	13	Others	134	154
Others	399	440	WISCONSIN	206	237
WEST VIRGINIA	215	237	Columbia	9	10
Greenbrier	12	13	Dane	17	20
Harrison	26	29	Dodge	11	13
Lewis	10	11	Fond du Lac	9	10
Monongalia	10	11	Rock	12	14
Monroe	12	13	Others	148	170
Others	145	160	MINNESOTA	151	166
NORTH CAROLINA	197	207	Blue Earth	6	7
Currituck	6	6	Faribault	7	8
Edgecombe	5	5	Fillmore	7	8
Greene	5	5	Freeborn	5	6
Lenoir	7	7	Martin	6	7

TURKEY CULTURE.

	1889	'96		1889	'96
Others	120	132	ALABAMA	178	187
IOWA	941	1129	Bullock	7	7
Dallas	16	19	Dallas	9	9
Davis	16	19	Lowndes	11	12
Greene	27	32	Montgomery	11	12
Linn	16	19	Wilcox	6	6
Polk	16	19	Others	134	141
Others	850	1021	MISSISSIPPI	194	204
MISSOURI	929	1022	Hinds	7	7
Audrain	23	25	Madison	6	6
Boone	24	26	Monroe	7	7
Callaway	22	24	Noxubee	7	7
Monroe	24	26	Panola	5	5
Pike	23	25	Others	162	170
Others	813	896	LOUISIANA	75	80
NEBRASKA	219	241	Avoyelles	3	3
Clay	8	9	De Soto	4	4
Gage	7	8	Ouachita	4	4
Lancaster	9	10	Rapides	3	3
Saline	6	7	St. Landry	5	5
York	6	7	Others	56	59
Others	183	201	TEXAS	536	643
KANSAS	530	583	Bell	12	14
Cowley	18	20	Ellis	12	14
Dickinson	18	20	Fayette	14	16
McPherson	13	14	Grayson	13	15
Marion	12	13	Lavaca	10	12
Sumner	15	17	Others	475	572
Others	454	499	ARKANSAS	119	125
KENTUCKY	672	706	Crawford	3	3
Bourbon	23	24	Jefferson	6	6
Harrison	25	26	Phillips	3	3
Madison	27	28	Sebastian	3	3
Mercer	20	21	Washington	6	6
Shelby	20	21	Others	98	103
Others	557	585	CALIFORNIA	288	360
TENNESSEE	430	452	Colusa	15	19
Bedford	22	23	Fresno	22	27
Giles	20	21	Sacramento	15	19
Lincoln	16	17	Tehama	17	21
Maury	20	21	Tulare	40	50
Rutherford	19	20	Others	179	224
Others	333	350			

THE TURKEY.

CHAPTER I.

THE TURKEY—ITS NATURAL HISTORY AND ORIGIN OF NAME.

BY E. RICHARDSON.

It is well known that the origin of the name of the domestic fowl called the turkey is involved in much obscurity. No dictionary that I know of gives its true etymology, but the name is supposed to arise from the belief that the bird came from the country of Turkey. It is the object of the present essay to trace the origin of the bird and its name, showing how the former came from the West and the latter from a far Eastern clime.

The origin of the turkey is, however, not nearly so uncertain as that of its name, for no fact of natural history is better established than that it was introduced into Europe from Mexico; and as to the date of the introduction, there can be as little doubt, for it is recorded by Prescott in his "Conquest of Mexico" that the followers of Cortez, soon after their landing, first met with this bird on their march to Cempoalla. It is told how they saw deer and various animals previously unknown to Europeans, and among them pheasants, and a species of peacock, as they described it, which was none other than the Wild turkey, the pride of the American forest and the progenitor of our proud and stately domestic fowl. The introduction of the bird into Europe naturally followed, as soon as circumstances permitted, and not long after,—for in the month of July, 1519, Cortez dispatched his "first letter" to his emperor,

Charles the Fifth, with a collection of fabrics, minerals, and other products of the New World. Three years later he dispatched another communication, together with a royal fifth of the spoils of Mexico, embracing a rich collection of all the products of the country, and it is not to be supposed that the turkey was omitted, especially as it was easily obtained. This consignment, however, was captured by a French privateer and fell into the hands of Francis the First, who is said to have gazed with wonder and envy upon the spoils of the Aztecs, and to have expressed the wish to see the clause in Adams' last will and testament that authorized his imperial rivals of Castile and Portugal to divide the New World between them.

Prescott further says, in describing the manners of the Mexicans: "The table was well supplied with substantial meats, especially game, of which the most conspicuous was the Wild turkey, erroneously supposed, as its name suggests, to have come originally from the East." He also says that this noble bird was introduced into Europe from Mexico, where it was domesticated, and was very common and abundant not only in Mexico, but all along the continent.

Thus we see how history records its introduction into Europe and refers to the error of supposing it to have come from the country so called. The Spaniards recognized its relation to the peacock by calling it *gallopavo*, the name of the true or Indian peacock being *pavon*. Naturalists place it in the same order in which are included pheasants, quail, etc. The peacock is the proud ornament of this order, and, as I have said, is a native of India, and is mentioned in the history of the East. History further tells us that the turkey was first brought to England in 1524, five years after Cortez first sent specimens to Spain. At first it was only in the hands of the rich, as naturally would be the case, but in course of time became accessible to the poor as well. So much, then, as to the origin of the bird itself, in which is shown how it is a native of Mexico, and was introduced into Europe by the expedition of Cortez to the New World, and called by his followers the "American" or "Mexican" peacock, from its habit of strutting.

Strange, then, how the bird came to be called turkey, a word in no way similar to the Anglo-Saxon *pawa*, the German *pfau*, the French *paon* or the Latin *pavo*, all names similar to one another and derived from the Latin, the bird having been brought from the East by the Romans. The mystery then is how, in view of all these facts, the name "turkey" came to be applied to this bird. It is obvious that we must look to some other language for a solution of the problem. Going to the far-off home of the peacock, we find in the Tamil language of India, a word *toka*, peacock, the primitive meaning of which refers to a train or trailing skirt. This word, adopted into the Hebrew language, becomes *tukki*, and by a slight change by the genius of the English language, becomes what we are looking for, *turkey*.

But, it is asked, How came it through the Hebrew? Let it be said, then, that at the time of the expedition of Cortez to Mexico, the despised and persecuted Jews were very numerous in Spain, and engaged, as they usually are, by their natural adaptability for gain, in merchandising. Their acuteness led them to deal in foreign birds, and curiosities and rarities, by which they reaped large profits, as these things were only purchased by the rich. Naturally, then, they saw in this new importation an opportunity for gain, which they seized, and as they used their own language as much as possible, it was not long before the Hebrew name for *peacock* became well known. Doubtless they designated it as the "American" peacock, for it was well known from whence it came. Thus it would be that the word *tukki* would constantly be heard in the market places, while the more scientific name of *pavo* would only be heard among the educated few, and so by force of numbers the name was used and anglicised into *turkey*, a name that gives rise to pleasant fancies about Thanksgiving day. Furthermore, the name was formerly spelled *turky*, as when Corbet, Bishop of Oxford, writes to Buckingham:

"Like very poore or counterfeit poore man, who, to preserve their *turky* or their hen, do offer up themselves."

In tracing the word to the Hebrew, the rules governing etymologies have been complied with, since here we have preserved the radicals t and k, which fact only tends to prove the origin of the word, according to the views herein set forth. And thus we see how the American peacock was introduced by Cortez to its gaudier Eastern rival, and received its ancient name, and how these proud birds of the Eastern and Western hemispheres became united to each other by a name which, traced backwards, reveals facts of linguistic interest, no less than the affinities and glories of earth's most important feathered tribes.

CHAPTER II.

THE WILD TURKEY (*Meleagris gallopavo*).

BY GEORGE ENTY.

Every American has heard of these birds, and not a few have seen them hanging in the market stalls of the large cities in some parts of the country, while a much smaller number have seen them alive in all the glory of their woody surroundings. And though he has never seen one alive or helped to kill or eat one, I believe there is not an American to-day who is not proud of this king of the forest. And well may we all be proud of our Wild turkeys, for of all of our useful birds it is the only one domesticated and made to serve our purpose to the fullest extent. Once found all along the Atlantic coast, all through the territory now known as Mexico and the Central American States, and in the great interior plain of North America, the turkey in a state of nature is to-day limited to the mountainous regions of New York and Pennslyvania, Virginia, the Carolinas, Tennessee, a few in Kentucky, some parts of the Gulf States, and rare sections of the Western States. Like all game, it is rapidly giving way to the incessant warfare of dogs, guns and hunters. The loggers go into the forest, followed soon by the farmer and his boys, and the poor turkeys lose their right to the land and to their claim on life. Thus it goes on all sides, and it will not be many years before they become almost as much of a rarity as a wild buffalo ranging his Western prairies. The habits of the turkey have not changed much by domestication. The bird has become less shy and timid, but hardly less watchful. It nests now along a fence, or in a bunch of weeds, grass or briers, where formerly it sought the most secluded spots along the mountain side. It roams with its young now in the wheat stubble, through the growing corn, and over the mown meadows and short-cropped pasture land, while its wild sister scratches among the leaves of the distant chestnut ridge, or gleans among the open oak glades for food. But although the first explorers of this continent found the turkey domesticated by some of the Indian tribes,' yet to this day many of the Wild traits show plainly in the common turkeys of the farm. And these latter probably have had no infusion of Wild blood for a hundred years, or more in many instances.

Wild turkeys in their native haunts are remarkably alert, cautious, and apparently possessed of a large share of reasoning powers. It is something wonderful, the manner in which they elude the oldest and most experienced hunters. My grandfather said that the whole countryside of gunners were out on the watch for a renowned albino gobbler that ranged the hills along the Allegheny river, in his young days, and although the spotless-white bird was frequently seen, on a bright morning or evening, flying from one hilltop to another, yet it was two or three years before he at last fell before the unerring aim of one of my grand uncles. And it was a source of much chagrin to my youngest brother, then a lad, not to be able to locate Minnehaha's nest the first season we had her. She was a full Wild hen, one year old, obtained from the mountains in central Pennsylvania, and was the beginning of our efforts at crossing Wild and Bronze turkeys, to improve the plumage and hardiness of the latter. But watch and trail her as he might, and with all the casual assistance a half-dozen brothers and sisters could give him, our turkey-hunting expert could not find the Wild hen's nest until after the poults were hatched and away. This, too, in a place where the woods were in small and isolated tracts. Early in the spring the largest and strongest gobbler drives off the weaker ones, and assumes a royal charge of the flock of hens about him. The young gobblers meekly stay with the flock until it breaks up for nesting; but any old gobblers in the flock leave it at once if they discover they cannot rule, and live in solitude, excepting that, attracted by his beauty, or perchance out of pity, or on account of some dislike for the ruling gobbler, some hen consorts with the banished bird, and shares his solitude. Again, two or three young gobblers will be found together, living in peace and plenty during the pleasant summer months. The nests are made exactly as the domesticated turkey's, and the number of eggs laid by one hen ranges from eight or nine to 18 or 20. The eggs are more thickly spotted with reddish-brown dots and blotches than those of tame turkeys or of all other than Bronze turkeys. They are not as large as domestic turkeys' eggs, yet a nest is occasionally found with eggs as large as White Holland eggs. If the eggs are taken from the nest and hatched under a domestic turkey, the young poults will run off to the forest as soon as hatched. This experiment in domestication was frequently tried by an uncle of the writer, who passed his youthful days in the midst of the finest Wild turkey county in Pennsylvania.

The little poults are very hardy, and, like quail and grouse, frequently mature without the loss of a single bird. The mother turkey takes most excellent care of her family, leading them slowly and carefully about the woods, turning over the dead leaves in search of worms, etc, and finding the wild berries in season, where the poults soon fill their little crops.

In late summer or autumn, several hens and their broods frequently go in one flock, and then, with some old gobbler as chief, whose plumage glistens like a leaf of gold, and emeralds, and garnets, and all the hues of the rainbow, they range the hills, plains, mountains and valleys in search of food. It is astonishing to the young hunter what an extended amount of territory a flock will travel in a day. I know a fast walker, while in the mountains a few years ago, who every Sabbath took his rifle and followed the trail of a large flock of Wild turkeys that kept along the mountain side, or on its summit. Yet this hunter never caught sight of the birds. A few lost feathers, and an extended list of ruffled grouse and squirrels that he could have shot had he not been expecting each minute to discover the turkeys, was all the reward he got for breaking the fourth commandment.

In autumn and early winter Wild turkeys are very plump and fat, and are the first game birds of the land. They are juicy and fat from long feeding on beechnuts, chestnuts, acorns, berries, and in the neighborhood of farms an occasional meal of wheat, corn, or buckwheat, the whole seasoned and spiced by the rich insects gathered in the forest, and made tender by the sharp frosts; and the purest meat food imaginable is produced by such constant living in the pure air and wood-scented forests, with the absence of all filth and vermin.

The painting of a Wild gobbler made by the great naturalist Audubon, is perhaps the best ever made, and will give a good idea of what a fine two-year-old gobbler is like. The hens are less brilliantly colored, but are finely marked, and the "rainbow tints" are more brilliant than the coloring on many Bronze gobblers seen at the fairs and poultry shows. My father shot an old gobbler which he thought would have weighed 25 lbs had it been fat. It was early in the spring, when turkeys are always lean. This bird, when cut up and salted, filled an empty powder keg. (Kegs hold 25 lbs of blasting powder.) A friend of ours in Mifflin county, Pa, raised a Wild gobbler which at maturity is said to have weighed 32 lbs. I think this weight was only estimated, and it is known that few people are correct judges of weight. And it may usually be taken with considerable allowance when weights of pure Wild hens are given much above 15 lbs, and gobblers above 20 lbs, while most hens weigh under 12 lbs and most gobblers under 16 lbs.

But, although when compared with large Bronze, White Holland, or Narragansett, the Wild turkey may appear small, its power to so reinforce the constitutional stamina of any turkeys with which it is crossed, and thus give progeny of superior size, is well known to many turkey raisers, while it is the only known way of retaining the brilliant marking so characteristic of well-bred Bronze turkeys. This fact should be better understood.

I can conceive of nothing more ornamental, taken all in all, than a stately Wild gobbler, with his beard almost touching the turf, his widespread tail with its black bars and rich chestnut edging, his trailing wings, the crimson and blue coloring of head and neck, and all the colors of sky, and sea, and autumn leaves glistening upon each feather—such a bird and his half-dozen mates strutting about the lawn and shrubbery of a gentleman's grounds. And no sight would be half as much appreciated by all lovers of nature as such an one. It would instinctively take the mind of the busy city resident back to his childhood on the farm; or, if so unfortunate as to have been born in town, back to his father's or mother's childhood, as oft related to him; back to the time when excitement ran high when the Wild turkeys were discovered feeding on the green wheat in spring; back to the great Thanksgiving hunt when father or brother brought in this noble chief of the wood to crown the feast; and back again to the long summer days spent roaming through the forest in search of juneberries, huckleberries, nuts, or wild grapes; and to the moment of supreme delight, when a flock of Wild turkeys suddenly start up from some hiding place, and with flashing eyes, spreading tails and notes of alarm walk away, slowly, a few steps, and then, with a rushing of brown leaves, like so many phantoms disappear in the dim light of the distant wood.

May the day never come when it shall be said the noble Wild turkey roams my native mountains no more.

THE WOOING OF THE WILD TURKEY.

BY J. M. MURPHY.

The males commence wooing as early as February in some of the extreme Southern States; but March is the opening of the love season throughout the country, and April the month in which it reaches its highest development. The males may then be heard calling to the females from every direction, until the woods ring with their loud and liquid cries, which are commenced long ere the sun appears above the horizon, and continue for hours with the steadiest persistency. As both sexes roost apart at this period, the hens avoid answering the gobblers for some time, but they finally become less obdurate, and coyly return the call. When the males hear this, all within hearing respond promptly and vehemently, uttering notes similar to those which the domestic gobblers do when they hear an unusual sound. If the female answering the call is on the ground, the males fly to her and parade before her with all the pompous strutting that characterizes the family. They spread and erect their tails, depress their wings with a quivering motion and trail them along the ground, and draw the head back on the shoulders, as if to increase their dignity and importance; then wheel, and march, and swell, and gobble, as if they were trying to outdo each other in airs and graces. The female, however, pays little attention to these ceremonious parades, and demurely looks on while the rivals for her affection try to outdo one another in playing the gallant and dandy. When the strutting and gobbling fail to win her, the candidates for matrimony challenge each other to mortal combat, and whichever is successful in the contest walks away with her in the most nonchalant manner. The easy indifference of the hen as to which she will follow may not be pleasing to persons imbued with romantic feelings, yet she is only obeying a wise law of nature, which decrees that only the fittest should live, and in the lower animal world these are necessarily chosen for their physical qualities.

The battles between the males are often waged with such desperate valor that more than one combatant is sent

FIG. 1. TRAP FOR WILD TURKEYS.

to join the great majority, as they deliver very heavy blows at each other's heads, and do not give up a contest until they are dead, or so thoroughly exhausted as to be scarcely able to move.

When one has killed another, it is said to caress the dead bird in an apparently affectionate manner, as if it were very sorry to have been compelled to do such a deed, but could not help it, owing to the force of circumstances; yet I have seen the winner in a tournament in such a rage that it not only killed its rival, but pecked out its eyes after it was dead. When the victors have won their brides they keep together until the latter commence laying, and then separate, for the males are so jealous that they would destroy the eggs if they could, in order to prolong the love period, and the hens, knowing this, carefully screen them. The males are often followed by more than one hen, but they are not so polygamous as their domestic congeners, as I never heard of a gobbler having more than two or three females under his protection. The adult gobblers drive the young males away during the erotic season, and will not even permit them to gobble if they can, so that the latter are obliged to keep by themselves, generally in parties of from six to ten, unless some of the veterans are killed, and then they occupy the vacated places of the bridegrooms, according to the order of their prowess.

Some aged males may also be found wandering through the woods in parties of two, three, four, or five, but they seldom mingle with the flocks, owing, apparently, to the waning of their salacious disposition. They are exceedingly shy and vigilant, and so wild that they fly immediately from an imaginary danger created by their own suspicious nature. They strut and gobble occasionally, but not nearly so much as do their younger kindred. Barren hens, which also keep by themselves, are almost as demonstrative in displaying their vocal powers, airs, and feathers as the old males, whereas they are exceedingly coy and unpretentious when fertile. This fact would seem to prove that ordinary animal nature is changed by circumstances. When the love season is over, the males are very much emaciated, so, when the hens leave them, they keep by themselves until they recover their strength, and then reunite in small bachelor parties; but, instead of being exceedingly clamorous, as they were in the early part of the mating period, they become almost silent. Yet they sometimes strut and gobble on their roosts, though, as a general rule, they do not, and content themselves with elevating and lowering the tail feathers, and uttering a puffing sound. They keep at this exercise for hours at a

FIG. 2. "CALLING" WILD TURKEYS.

time on moonlight nights, without rising from their perch, and sometimes continue it until daylight.

When the hen is ready to lay, she scratches out a slight hollow in a thicket, a canebrake, beside a prostrate tree, in tall grass or weeds, or a grain field, and lines it rudely with grass or leaves, and then deposits her eggs in it.

These, which vary in number from ten to twenty, are smaller and more elongated than those of the domestic turkey, and are of a dull-cream or a dirty-white color, sprinkled with brownish-red spots. Audubon says that several hens may lay their eggs in one nest, and hatch them and raise the broods together. He found three hens siting on forty-two eggs in a single nest, and one was always present to protect them.

If the eggs are not destroyed, only one brood is raised in a year; but if they are, the female calls loudly for a male, and when she is rejoined by one, both keep company until she is ready to commence laying again, when she deserts him or drives him away, as he has the very strongest penchant for destroying the eggs, in order to keep her in his company. This forces her to build her nest in the most secluded spot she can find, and to cover it carefully with leaves or grass whenever she leaves it. We present pictures showing how Wild turkeys are "called" by hunters to them with whistles, and how they are entrapped. When once enticed within this trap, they are so confused as to be unable to find their way out. Fig 1 makes the trap plain. An inclined path or trench is arranged, which deepens gradually and ends inside the pen. Corn is strewn over the bottom of the trench, the turkeys follow along head down led by the corn until they are inside, and then with heads up they see no way out.

CHAPTER III.

THE BREEDS OF TURKEYS.

There is less variation in the ordinary domestic turkey than among common fowls, not so many being kept, and more care being taken to keep them pure. The following classification may be considered as correct and is accepted by breeders:—

The Wild
- Mexican
- Honduras
- North American

The Domesticated
- American Mammoth Bronze
- White Holland
- Narragansett
- Black
- Buff
- Slate or Lavender

The *Mexican* is generally considered to be the progenitor of the common domesticated turkey, as is fully set forth.

The *Honduras* or *Ocellated* turkey, found in Central America, appears to have baffled all attempts to domesticate and rear it outside the tropics. It is said to possess a plumage equal in brilliancy to that of the peacock, and also to have the feathers of its tail "ocellated," or eyed.

The *North American* Wild turkey resembles the Mexican in color, but rivals it in size. It is a somewhat longer bird than the domesticated variety, and differs from it in an absence of pure white in any of its feathers, the pencilings of its wings and the dull white or gray of its tail being of a chestnut color. Our second chapter treats in detail of this superb progenitor of the useful domestic turkey. Audubon's fine painting is still the best portraiture of this noble bird, and from it our frontispiece is produced. The Wild turkey is still of the most importance to breeders, because fresh infusion of pure, wild blood into our breeding stock seems to be necessary, to prevent decadence of vitality, and to insure thrift and health in our improved breeds—that is, for those who raise turkeys for market.

THE BRONZE TURKEY.

H. S. BABCOCK.

The Bronze is the largest variety among our turkeys. The standard weights are: For cock 32 lbs, cockerel 24 lbs, hen 22 lbs, and pullet 15 lbs. These weights, though high, are often exceeded by the birds. Forty pounds and even more are reached by the old toms, and we know of one hen turkey which weighed, when we saw her, twenty-nine pounds, and her owner expected her to reach thirty pounds in a short time.

There is some obscurity about the origin of this variety, although there is reason to believe that it resulted from crossing the Wild turkey, the original of all the domesticated varieties, upon the Black turkey. Early references to the variety show that it was at first known as the "Black Bronzed," but the term was too long and it became shortened into Bronze. This variety is interesting as showing that, after a marked departure from the early color, it has come back to very nearly the color of its Wild original. The Black had departed a long distance from the rich hues of the Wild turkey, but the lines are restored in the Bronze variety.

The male has a long head, with good breadth of skull, the rich red skin being carunculated. The strong beak is well curved, and is of the color known as horn, darkest at the base and growing light as it approaches the tip. The eyes are dark-hazel in color, contrasting with the rich red of the face and jaws. The wattle, or snout, is of the same color as the face and of good size, and hangs down from above. The long curving neck is clothed in plumage of rich bronze. The back of the male, starting from its junction with the neck, rises in a gentle curve to about the center, which is the highest point, and then descends to the tail. The feathers are of the richest bronze, each ending in a narrow band of black, and in the sunlight they are indescribably beautiful. The broad, full and prominent breast is covered with plumage of dark bronze. The body is long, well rounded, and midway of its length quite deep, and the feathers are black with bronze shadings, less lustrous, though beautiful, than those upon the back and breast. In fact, in almost all fowls kept by man, the top plumage is much the richest, and is so, probably, because of the effects of the sun upon it. Even in varieties which are supposed to be uniform in coloring, like the Buff Cochin, the upper plumage is much the richest in coloring. The wings have a wide spread, and the muscles are strong enough to enable the heavy bird to rise to a considerable hight from the ground. The primary feathers, when the wing is opened, are seen to be black or nearly so, with more or less regular penciling of gray or white. The secondaries are like the primaries but as one counts from the primaries, they are seen to have more and more brown and bronze, and less and less of white or gray. The wing bows are black with a rich greenish or bronzy luster, and the coverts are similar in color, each ending in a broad band of black that makes a bar across the wings. The long tail consists of feathers the ground color of which is black, and across which are irregularly placed narrow bands of light brown, terminating in a broad band of black with a wide gray margin. The tail coverts do not differ materially from the main feathers of the tail, except that as they approach the back they grow richer in bronze shadings. The stout thighs, of good length, are clad in dark, bronze-colored feathers, and the shanks, which are long and stout in bone, are in immature birds almost black, but in adult birds they become flesh-colored. This fact will enable one to decide with some certainty upon the age of a turkey.

2

As the female is colored very much the same as the male, it will be unnecessary to describe her markings in detail. But it is to be noted that the lines of the female are never so rich as those of the male, that the markings are apt to be less distinct, and that the margins of the feathers are, as a rule, gray in color. Considered by herself the female would be considered a very handsome bird, but regarded in connection with her more richly colored mate, she has a very sober and modest dress, as becomes her sex.

The Bronze is the most popular variety among turkeys, due probably to its great size, and perhaps also due in some measure to its increased hardiness, secured by the infusion of Wild blood in its origin. At any rate, whatever be the cause, the Bronze turkey is bred very largely, and more largely than any other variety.

Mr Barber adds: "When the golden sun is slowly sinking in the sky, what lovelier sight can meet the eye than a flock of brilliant-hued Bronze turkeys, as they homeward plod their weary way, to eat and drink, to roost, and perchance to dream of the fat grasshoppers they will find on the morrow."

JUDGING BRONZE TURKEYS.

BY GEORGE WOLFF.

[We presume the average reader will be interested to know that Mr Wolff, although a paralytic since infancy, is one of the most experienced breeders and judges of turkeys. His being a cripple has made him a close student in his work, and we believe he has a more exact knowledge of the Bronze breed and its markings and qualifications than any living person.]

This exceedingly popular breed of Turkeys challenges the admiration of all, with its lustrous plumage, strutting carriage and prodigious size. It is, by all odds, the most hardy breed of turkeys yet introduced. The standard weight for Bronze turkeys is: Cock 32 lbs, hen 20 lbs, cockerel 24 lbs, pullet 15 lbs. Some 15 or 20 years since, such weights were considered enormous. But the majority of the Bronze turkeys that are now found in our best breeders' yards exceed the above weights. It has been my pleasure, on several occasions during the past few years, to see, at our best exhibitions, adult toms turn the balance at 38 to 45 lbs, and hens 24 to 32 lbs. If breeders will only continue to mate for great size, the day is not far distant when we will see birds of even a greater weight.

In judging, I am a strong advocate of specialty judges. It is ripe knowledge in any business that prepares a person for a successful undertaking. I do not believe there is a professional judge on the face of the earth who can successfully compare or score the several different classes of fowls he is sure to find at most of our exhibitions. Turkeys, particularly, often suffer, as many of our professional judges reside in cities and never saw a turkey, except in the show pen or at their Thanksgiving dinner.

Great size and weight is the most necessary element of a Bronze turkey. No matter how fine a specimen may be in plumage, if it lacks size it drops back to nothing but a mongrel.

To get the symmetry of a turkey in judging, is often quite a tedious undertaking. It may require considerable patience and coaxing to get the bird to stand in proper position, especially if it is a young bird that has never been exhibited. A model show specimen should be moderately tall and very rangy, evenly proportioned and well balanced in all shape sections and very sturdy in appearance.

The color of the male turkey's head may change during excitement, but when in a natural condition it should be bright red, the corunculations extending well down on neck, with a large, well-developed wattle. When scoring I find but few judges who pay any attention to color or shape of head. This is a mistake, as many specimens are faulty in color and shape, and should suffer a cut of one-half to one, according to the defect.

The back must be well curved and of good width. Many specimens are faulty in the back, being too straight and

FIG. 3. THE PRIZE BRONZE TURKEY.

This bird won the grand prize offered by the New York fanciers' club some years ago. He was two years old, weighed forty-five pounds, and was bred by Sherman Hartwell, of Connecticut. With seven fine hens, he was bought by William Simpson, and exhibited at numerous poultry shows in England, capturing prizes in every case, and proving superior to any English-bred turkeys. The fine picture we present is from an instantaneous photograph by Smalls, taken for the *American Agriculturist*, and drawn by Keeler.

narrow. The breast must be full and nicely rounded, but not to drop so low as to injure the form, as is sometimes seen in aged toms.

If a specimen is really brilliant in color, there is but little chance to cut till you get to wing, back and tail, and sometimes legs. The primary wing feathers must be black, or nearly so, each feather to be evenly penciled with white or gray bars. Many Bronze turkeys are very faulty in primary color, as those feathers are very apt to be too dull and irregular in penciling, especially as we near the quill ends of those feathers. The secondary feathers are not so clearly defined, and usually have a narrow edging of white or gray on the outside web of feathers. As you leave the center of secondary feathers, and count up towards the back, the color rapidly changes to a bronzy brown, which has more or less luster when seen in the sunlight. Occasionally we find a specimen with solid black feathers, and sometimes several of them in primary or secondary feathers. They should be punished by heavy cutting. It is a grand wing, indeed, that escapes with an honest cut of one point.

The standard calls for a black tail irregularly penciled with narrow bands of light brown. It is a mistaken idea for a judge to think a Bronze turkey must have a fully penciled tail, for I find that brown predominates over the black in most every instance with such tails, and if a person continues to breed from birds with fully penciled tails, we soon destroy the black band on tail covert, that is so much admired by true Bronze turkey fanciers. Again, I will say that where we use so much penciling we lighten the color of thigh in many specimens, and I would advise judges to be more lenient with tails containing less penciling.

Many years since, I discovered white penciling under the tail covert on the main tail feathers of many Bronze turkeys. It usually confines itself to two or four of the center feathers, and sometimes extends the entire length of the tail feathers. It usually keeps out of sight from the ordinary observer by not extending beyond the covert. The markings are similar to those of primary wing feathers, but are usually not so decided in white. I have examined flock after flock for this defect, and find it every time. This defect should be punished without mercy, and, I am ashamed to say, many of our best breeders and judges have never discovered it. Can you blame me for asking for specialty judges? We often find the edging to tail covert and lesser coverts, as they extend up the back, to be cinnamon in color. It denotes Wild blood and should be cut as a defect, as such edging should be of a dull white or gray.

It is seldom that we find young turkeys as brilliant or clean in wing color as aged birds. The female is like the male in color, only not so clear or brilliant, and the breast feathers must be edged with dull white, or gray. If breeders and judges will only accept my advice, they will find I am leading them to the brink of success.

THE BLACK TURKEY.

H. S. BABCOCK.

It is quite probable that the Black turkey was produced from the domesticated Wild, either by continuously selecting the blackest specimens, those showing the least tendency toward bands, or that through melanism a black specimen or specimens sported from the common kind, and became the foundation of this variety. The Black is a long-established variety. In certain parts of England it was, until quite recently, the favorite variety, and is known there as the Black Norfolk, having been long bred in Norfolk. The introduction of the Bronze turkey into England has done considerable, in recent years, to depose it of its quondam supremacy. The Black is a handsome variety. All black fowls are handsome, American prejudices to the contrary notwithstanding. Black plumage means black beak and legs, or approximately so, with white skin. Black is the most lustrous plumage we have. In the sun-

FIG. 4. "PURE-BLOODED" BLACK TURKEYS.

light the greens and purples are extremely beautiful. But black in this country, owing to unreasoning prejudice, is not a popular color. Only one black variety of fowls is widely popular—the Langshan. The Minorca narrowly escapes being popular. But black ought to be popular, for its wearers are usually hardy and always beautiful. So, with this prejudice in view we need not wonder that Black turkeys are comparatively few in number. The Black turkey should be black throughout. The American standard makes "feathers other than black" a disqualification. But despite this rigidity, the variety often "harks back" to its banded ancestors, and bands will show on wing feathers and tail. These bands do not hurt the flavor of the flesh, although they may prevent the bird from winning a prize. If the breeders of Black turkeys will fatten all that show these bands—marks of heredity—and use only the solid-colored specimens for breeders, this tendency will be reduced, though it is impossible to predict how many generations it will take to obliterate it wholly.

The Black is a much smaller bird than the Bronze, and appears to have deteriorated in size, possibly owing to the breeders of this variety sacrificing the best birds at Thanksgiving and Christmas for market, instead of retaining them for stock. Some of the chicks have a little white about the head. The adult male should weigh twenty-five pounds or more, the hen twelve pounds.

WHITE HOLLAND TURKEYS.
GEORGE ENTY.

A breed that is less widely known than the popular Bronze turkey is the White Holland, or White turkey, as it is called for short, yet birds of this breed are kept in considerable numbers in some sections, and are becoming better known, and each year more frequently seen among turkeys in the shows and in the market. Like everything else on this sphere, they have their good qualities and also their weak points. But most persons, after keeping them a few years, declare them to be the finest possible breed of turkeys, and would on no account dispose of their flocks and change the breed. But, after making due allowance for all over-description of the breed and its doings, it must be admitted that it is worthy of a very prominent place among domestic fowls.

The origin of this breed of turkeys is in doubt, and the name is not a correct index to the locality of their origin. They came probably from selecting the finest white turkeys found among the flocks, and by continuously mating these white birds, a race of such fowls could be obtained in time to breed true to this characteristic. But it has been in America, and within the last 12 or 15 years, that the greatest progress in developing the breed has been made. The standard weights of this breed are as follows: Cock 26 lbs, cockerel 16 lbs, hen 16 lbs, and pullet 10 lbs, —lower weights than are required for any other breed. This would naturally lead one unacquainted with the breed to suppose it to be quite small. On the contrary, I have seen numbers of cocks weighing 30 to 33 lbs, hens 17 to 19 lbs, cockerels 18 to 22 lbs, and pullets 13 to 16 lbs, showing conclusively that the standard weights are too low. Mr Peter Enty, who has had considerable experience with these fowls, writes under recent date: "I dressed a young gobbler last fall, six months and six days old, that weighed 16 1-2 lbs dressed for market, and he was the nicest looking bird I ever saw. His skin was transparent white, as was the flesh, and with his red head, and the white neck feathers down to his beard and wing, tail and fluff feathers on, he was a sight that would attract attention in any first-class market." Such a weight at six months reveals the possibilities of large size and heavy weights in this breed if people would try to bring them out.

Perhaps one reason why this breed has not been made larger and heavier is because with the size as it now is, they are just suited for ordinary family use. The largest breeds are too large for most families, hence the smaller breeds command readier sale. The great 40 to 46 lb toms must be sold on the holidays or Thanksgiving market if sold at all. A plump young turkey dressing 8 to 15 lbs will sell readily at almost any season. Certainly the same size can be had in any of the breeds, or with the common stock of the farms, but not so readily, as a rule. I have on several occasions seen large flocks of Bronze turkeys of a uniform size in which the hens weighed about 10 or 12 lbs, and the males 15 or 16 lbs at Thanksgiving. White Holland turkeys have been so often extolled for their domesticity, that it seems almost like sacrilege to tell a different tale. And yet, after keeping several of the best-known breeds for years, as well as the subject of this sketch, I find that there is little if anything to choose between the several breeds on the score of tameness. It has frequently been said that White Hollands are weakly and hard to raise, but I have known instances where every egg of a clutch hatched, and every poult lived to maturity. A correspondent says: "They must be hardy, or I could never have raised any last year on this place, which is so damp and cold that it is unfit to raise geese, or much less a tender thing like a turkey." But hardy as I believe them, let no one expect to find them of whalebone or iron, for they are not. They will die if exposed to too much cold and dampness, just like any other turkeys; they must be kept free from lice, or they droop and die like any fowl; and they must be fed proper food in proper quantities, or they will never live to grace a Thanksgiving table, or call forth words of praise at the Christmas festive board. Then, too, it must be remembered by all who should attempt to raise White turkeys, that if hardy poults are wanted the breeding stock must be hardy, well matured, properly kept, and not closely related. More weak poults come into the world to **worry their** owners during **a brief existence,** on account

THE BREEDS OF TURKEYS.

FIG. 5. PURE-BRED WHITE HOLLAND TURKEYS.

of close breeding and poor selection of breeding stock, than from any natural weakness in the fowls as a breed.

White Holland turkeys are perhaps the best layers among turkeys. It is sometimes reckoned as a fault that few hens want to hatch early in the season, and a large number of eggs and no broody hens is not an uncommon occurrence. This is no doubt the result of selection, as I have found the progeny of a remarkably good or poor layer was of much the same nature as regards prolificness. And again I have seen hens of this breed hatch twice in one season; others become broody before laying a dozen eggs, and three times ere they had laid the second dozen; while others were hard to "break up" when once broody. A friend kept four hens a few years since which laid 204 eggs during the season, one hen hatching and rearing a brood in July.

Are they beautiful? That is a matter of taste only. I may think so, or may class some other breed above them for beauty, while you will be of the opposite opinion.

Therefore I say nothing on this point. I believe them to be a good turkey and worthy of the best efforts of breeders and farmers in general, and think no one need be seriously disappointed in them if he goes ahead properly and knows what he is doing. Truthful pictures have been practically unknown heretofore, but in the accompanying engraving from nature of prize-winning White Hollands, our artist reproduces on printed page a spirited but lifelike view of these beautiful birds. "The White Hollard turkeys are bred in large numbers and when prepared for the table are considered the finest flavored turkey we have, but are less hardy than other breeds."

THE BUFF TURKEY.

H. S. BABCOCK.

Among the rarer varieties of the turkey is the Buff. Just why this color should be rare is not plain to understand, for few colors are more pleasing to the eye. If it lacks the brilliant reflections of the Bronze or the iridescence of the Black, it has a beauty all its own, which quite compensates for this lack. Delicate colors are not necessarily indications of delicate constitutions. We have, it is true, long been influenced by the impression that

FIG. 6. BUFF TURKEY COCK.

white fowls are less hardy than colored ones, but this impression would not apply to buff. The buff-colored turkey is no more delicate than its darker cousins.

How it perhaps originated can be guessed, though we have no records to tell us the matings or the maker of the matings. But, as black-red domestic fowls crossed upon white often produce an approximation to buff, which, by selection, can be perfected, we believe that a cross of the Bronze and the White turkey, with subsequent selection, would produce the Buff variety. In fact, many Buff turkeys show quite plainly the marks of such an ancestry. A variety of the Buff turkey used to be bred in Pennsylvania, under the name of Tuscawara Reds. These birds had a deeper plumage than the ordinary Buff and resembled it very much as a Rhode Island Red resembles a Buff Plymouth Rock. We have not heard much about the Tuscawara Reds lately, and presume, therefore, that they did not "catch on" to the public fancy.

The standard weights of Buff turkeys are somewhat less than for the Bronze and Narragansett. A comparison of these, with the White, will show fairly well how these birds average in weight relation to each other.

	Bronze. lbs.	Narragansett. lbs.	Buff. lbs.	White. lbs.
Adult cock,	35	32	27	26
Young cock,	24	22	18	16
Adult hen,	20	22	18	16
Young hen,	15	14	12	10

The Black and Slate varieties are of the same weight as the Buff. The somewhat less weight of the Buff turkey when compared with the Bronze or the Narragansett, perhaps will account, in part at least, for its less popularity, for big birds catch the eye, and people forget that sometimes the smaller birds are quite as profitable to rear, and actually sell better than the big ones. Not long ago the writer noticed that the market quotations for turkeys dressing from eight to ten pounds were higher than for those of greater weight. The manager of the Anowon Farm recently told the writer that their turkeys—all Whites—had sold well, the price being thirty-five cents per pound.

However originated, and whether popular or not, the Buff turkey is one of the most beautiful varieties we have.

The rich red of its head and exposed neck, its white, or flesh colored, shanks, and its pure buff plumage, fading into light cream on the wings, harmonize perfectly and make its color scheme truly artistic. But, and here, we opine, is the real difficulty, buff is a difficult color to breed perfectly, and among Buff turkeys, as well as among Buff fowls, there will be too much white or too much black in the plumage. The result will be that out of many birds but a few will possess the desired color characteristics. But if one rears the Bronze, nearly every specimen will be colored aright and the flock will possess the desired uniform appearance.

THE SLATE TURKEY.

These differ from the Buff mainly in the color of the plumage. They are good market birds, and when in prime condition make a handsome appearance in the show pen. The variety is also called Blue, Maltese or Lavender.

THE NARRAGANSETT TURKEY.

H. S. BABCOCK.

The name of this variety is derived from the beautiful bay that extends from Newport to Providence, in the state of Rhode Island. It is the variety which, in all probability, first gave to Rhode Island turkeys their world-wide reputation. That reputation has remained, though the variety has, to a considerable extent, disappeared from the borders of the bay. The greater size of the Bronze turkey has been a potent cause in the gradual disappearance of other varieties. Yet the Narragansett is by no means a small variety,—it is nearly as large as the Bronze. The standard weights are: For cock thirty-two pounds, for cockerel and hen twenty-two pounds each, and for pullet fourteen pounds, and are the heaviest weights given to any variety except the Bronze. These weights are not

FIG. 7. NARRAGANSETT TURKEYS.

extreme, for they are often exceeded, although a thirty-two-pound turkey is a large bird.

The Narragansett turkey has a striking plumage. The feathers of the neck, back, breast and body may be described as deep black, terminating with a broad light-gray band margined with black. The large wings have black bows, which show a bronzy luster in the sunshine; the flight feathers, including both primaries and secondaries, are black, or nearly black, barred with white or gray; and the wings, when folded, show two distinct narrow bars across them. The tail feathers are black, barred irregularly with brown, and end in a broad black band margined with white or gray, generally a very light gray. The shanks and toes are, in color, a deep salmon or brown. The plumage of both sexes is the same, except that the plumage of the male is more distinct in its markings and deeper in color. The female is the lighter colored specimen, its gray being usually of a paler shade.

This coloring makes the Narragansett a distinguished looking bird. The contrast between its black and its gray causes the markings to stand out well, and the effect is extremely pleasing to the eye. There are not wanting those who believe that this coloration is really more beautiful than that of the magnificent Bronze, with its richer lines and more abundant luster.

The size of the variety and its attractive coloring are sufficient reasons for a desire to have it more extensively bred than it is. It has a sufficient degree of hardiness and the other practical qualities, to warrant a renewed interest in one of the best varieties of the turkey. It certainly ought to become more common in its original home, and not allow so many birds really inferior to it to occupy its place.

The Narragansetts are not so large as the Mammoth Bronze. Their plumage is a metallic black, each feather terminating in a broad, light steel-gray band, edged with black. These birds are popular in southern New England, where they are extensively grown for the city markets. They are hardy and as easily reared as the Mammoth Bronze. The Narragansetts have thick set, plump bodies, and short legs, are quick growers, mature early, and do not roam as far from home as Bronze turkeys.

THE BRUSH TURKEY.
BY FRANKLANE L. SEWELL.

In the zoological gardens of London, the Brush turkey has made its nest, as it does in its wild state, by constructing a crude mound of earth, leaves, grass, sand, and other materials that were at hand, which, by fermentation, becomes heated. The eggs are deposited therein. Instead of a mother turkey on her nest, the picture of patience, is to be seen the female in apparent carelessness strolling about the inclosure. The cock seems the most interested, and by far the busier one of the pair. Not a sign of herbage, not even a straw, is to be seen on the ground of their runway, except what is contained in the mound. The male bird, for it is he who constructs the mound nest and keeps it constantly in correct condition, has apparently worn and torn every bit of herbage from the ground, in his dragging and scratching materials toward the huge pile, which is about five feet high and eight or more feet across the base.

While I stood sketching these strange birds, the male nervously ran to and from the mound, once in a while scratching the materials at the base towards the top, and several times I saw him peck at and drive the female from the place, as if in fear she might disturb something. The superintendent of the gardens, in a very interesting account of the Brush turkey, says that when the young are hatched they creep from the mound, stout and strong, ready to care for themselves, and on the second or third day are capable of flight; that they are quite unnoticed by

either of the parent birds and apparently careless of each other, hunting their own food, and each selecting, regardless of the others, his shelter or roosting-place for the night. These birds apparently have no relationship to the true American turkey, but are inserted here as a matter of interest.

THE BEST BREED.

The Bronze turkeys are at present the favorites with the majority of those who grow turkeys for the market. Size and hardiness are the important factors which cause this favoritism. Sometimes private customers prefer white- or yellow-skinned ones, just as they prefer yellow-legged chickens. Boston has made the present taste in New England, which decidedly prefers yellow-legged chickens, and though the preference is not emphatic for the skin of White Hollands, yet, doubtless, it is because it is difficult to obtain them. The compiler of this book has sold yellow-legged and yellow-skinned poultry at fifty per cent advance on the price of dark-legged chickens. It may be a fancy, but if you get your money, what matters it? By persisting in raising white turkeys for the New England market for a series of years, a demand may be made for them. Outside of New England, unless we may except the Philadelphia market, the color of the skin and legs of a fowl or turkey receives but little consideration.

COMMON TURKEYS.

By "common" turkeys is meant mongrels,—all sorts of breeds mixed. Too many farmers have such flocks. Get a first-rate male of the variety you want and mate him with your hens. From their progeny select the best females, and mate them with a fine male of the same breed, but not related to their sire. Pursue this course, "grading up," for two or three years, and you will have as good a flock as you need for market purposes.

THE BREEDS OF TURKEYS.

INFUSING FRESH BLOOD FROM WILD TURKEYS.

[From reports of the Rhode Island Agricultural Experiment Station, where this matter has been the object of much research and experimenting.]

"Where wild turkeys are plenty, crosses between wild and domestic birds frequently occur without design on

FIG. 9. WILD BLOOD TURKEYS.

From photographs of stock at the Rhode Island Experiment Station.

the part of the owner of the latter. Scores of cases are recorded where a wild gobbler from the woods has taken possession of a flock of common turkeys, sometimes after first battling with and killing the domestic gobbler. The results of such a cross in almost every case have been so satisfactory that such matings are much desired by turkey raisers in those sections, and young wild birds are caught for this purpose and brought up with common young turkeys. Very often nests of wild turkey eggs are found in the woods and hatched on the farm. These domesticated wild birds usually persist in roosting separate from the others, generally in the woods or on the top of a house or barn. When raised from the egg they become more gentle and fearless than the domestic turkey, but if chased or frightened they recover their wild habits very quickly. Wild turkey crosses are hardier and healthier than common turkeys, and rarely have disease. Half-blood hens are generally too wild, but half-blood gobblers are not as wild and are suitable for crossing with domestic hens. A small proportion of wild blood improves the size, form, and general appearance, as well as the vigor, without being a disadvantage in any way. A quarter-wild cross is better, for practical breeding, than a pure wild or half-wild bird. Half-wild crosses do well if allowed a large range, but are not well suited for woody countries or as easily kept on small places as the domestic turkey. Wild turkey hens under domestication and wild first-cross hens often disappear in the spring and are not seen until fall, when they usually return to their own home with a brood of nearly full-grown turkeys. Half-blood mothers make their young too wild. Half-bloods reared by domestic turkey hens are not much inclined to stray. Quarter-bloods, under certain conditions, may be as wild as the wild bird of the woods."

The wild blood gives the cross an astonishing ability to care for themselves. It is apt to have the strongest influence in breeding. If first crosses are bred together, the stock resembles the pure wild, and after several generations cannot be distinguished from the pure wild by good judges. The older the bird grows the more he shows the wild blood. Crosses have much of the superior game flavor of the wild, and command a higher price for the table. The half or one-fourth wild are active, hardy, and unusually heavy and firm in flesh. They may attain great size, but will prove specially popular because they will produce poults weighing ten to twelve pounds the first autumn after they are hatched, and thus make a most popular market bird. The Rhode Island Experiment Station has found this invest-

FIG. 10. PURE WILD GOBBLER BRED IN CONFINEMENT.
By courtesy of the Rhode Island Agricultural Experiment Station. Reproduced from colored plates in Wright's Illustrated Book of Poultry.

ment of wild blood so beneficial that it has obtained wild stock and distributed half-wild gobblers all over the State. This is having a most beneficial effect, unless the turkeys are so bred as to make the proportion of wild blood greater than one-fourth. In that case they are sometimes wilder and smaller than is desired for practical purposes. Read the experience in the latter part of this book, of Mr. Tucker of Prudence Island with three-eighths wild turkeys, fully confirming the above. These birds were not tame but were managed all right, and of those hatched more lived than of any other lot Mr. Tucker has ever had, and they were larger, more uniform in size, ate heartier, fatted quicker and were plumper and handsomer when dressed.

Some wild Bronze crosses that are half and three-fourths wild blood, are occasionally as large as the pure Bronze turkeys. Several years' crossing, however, with the selections of the largest for breeding each season, gives the greatest size. See Fig. 11 for an illustration of this fact. Wild and wild-cross birds, especially the hens, owing to their slim heads and necks and their having less red about the head, are, when seen among common turkeys, often taken for sick birds by those not familiar with them. Half-wild crosses are very hardy, but smaller than domestic turkeys, and the hens roam so much and steal their nests so far from home, that they are undesirable in breeding for market purposes. They often roam off and stay away all summer, but are almost sure to return in the fall. Their flesh is about as fine as that of a wild turkey. Half-wild gobblers are more manageable than the hens, and just the thing to cross with common turkeys. The birds raised from such a mating are not only of good size, but hardy and thrifty, and make fine dressed turkeys.

The gobbler has the most influence on size of progeny. It will not do to coop wild-cross hens, as they thrash about and kill their young in their attempts to escape. It is to be hoped that the time when wild turkeys are to become extinct is far distant. The methods followed by the average turkey raiser so depreciate the stock that, without the occasional introduction of fresh, hardy blood from the forest, it would become very much degenerated. When there are no wild turkeys except those preserved by man, the salvation of the domestic turkey will depend on fanciers—those who breed for beauty and utility. They maintain the varieties pure and perfect them. They, only, expend the required time and money, and follow the laws of breeding necessary to prevent the

THE BREEDS OF TURKEYS. 41

FIG. 11. PART WILD BLOOD BRONZE TURKEY.

This bird, Eureka, was from a thoroughbred Bronze hen, while his sire had one-fourth wild blood. At sixteen months he weighed thirty-six pounds, and at twenty-eight months tipped the scales at forty-eight and one-half pounds, winning first prizes both years at New England and York State poultry shows. The accession of wild blood only three removes back, even if it added nothing to the great weight of this bird, unquestionably contributed to its vitality and the brilliancy of its plumage.

stock from running out. When will farmers, generally, appreciate the value of such service and cease to scoff at fancy prices?

STANDARD OF EXCELLENCE.

The American standard of excellence gives the following scale of points for turkeys, by which judges determine the qualifications of exhibition birds: Symmetry 10, weight 30, condition 10, head 5, wattle 5, neck 5, back 7, breast and body 10, wings 8, tail 5, legs 5, total 100.

CHAPTER IV.

TURKEY GROWING AS A BUSINESS.

Not every one can engage in the turkey business as an occupation or means of livelihood, because so much is dependent upon surroundings. All farmers are not so situated that they can raise turkeys without incommoding their neighbors. The laws of trespass are rigid in most States, and any neighbor who objects to your birds roaming over his fields can make you trouble, if he be so disposed. Turkeys must have range, and if your own fields are not wide enough to allow them that necessary element of success, either be sure of your neighbors' good nature, or do not embark in the business at all. Many turkey-growers believe that turkeys have a perversity of disposition, which impels them to leave their own premises, where there is plenty of room, grain and grasshoppers, and trespass on some neighbor's land, to get less food.

A few turkeys can be grown on a small farm; but there are plenty of abandoned farms in New England, which can be bought for the price of the buildings alone, large enough to grow large flocks. The convenience to large markets enhances the profits. In the Western and Southern States still greater numbers may be kept, owing to wider ranges and cheapness of grain. Common fowls, with proper care, can be kept with profit in any city or village lot, but centuries of domestication have not changed the turkeys' natural love for a necessity of free range. They can be made tame by gentleness; they learn to be familiar with those who care for them, and can be taught to come home every night; but, as soon as they have left the stage of "infancy," as shown by "shooting the red," their propensity to wander in search of their food asserts itself, and they must have that privilege or they will sicken and die. This is a fortunate trait, for two reasons. First, it makes the bird's flesh better food for man; second, it limits the business to fewer persons, who get paying prices for their labor. If turkeys could be raised at a profit in confinement, their flesh would not be so wholesome, and so many people would go into the business that the

FIG. 12. WHITE HOLLAND TURKEYS.
From a photograph of a Rhode Island flock.

price would come down to a non-paying point. Turkey nature itself effectually prevents all danger of overdoing the business.

Turkeys are not hard to raise after you know how. For the first few weeks of their lives they require more care than any other domesticated bird, but after they are fully feathered and have "thrown the red," they require less care than any other fowl. It requires but little capital

Houses, except in the extreme North, and turkey sheds in other sections, are not needed. Turkeys must be raised on farms, and farmers raise much of the grain they need. One tom and three to five hen turkeys are enough to begin with. When you can raise all, or nearly all, of their progeny, then it will be time to think of enlarging your business. From a flock of six you ought to raise seventy-five to one hundred turkeys.

Turkey raising is an excellent business for women. Many a farmer's wife, whose husband does not care to "bother with poultry," can earn from fifty to three hundred dollars a year, according to the size of the flock, the range and the market, without seriously impeding the other necessary work which falls to the lot of farmers' wives.

It is unnecessary to quote market prices here as a criterion, for they vary so in different localities. In 1894, for Thanksgiving and Christmas, turkeys retailed in Indianapolis for ten to twelve cents per pound; in Boston, from eighteen to twenty-five cents, according to quality. Whoever engages in turkey raising must remember that success in raising turkeys is bought at the same price as liberty—eternal vigilance.

Rhode Island Experiment Station: "To the foregoing it should be said, that we have found the largest and most thrifty looking turkeys on rather light land, and where new blood is frequently introduced. If a flock becomes diseased, the land which they wander over may become contaminated, and affect other flocks which occupy the same ground, hence it is sometimes necessary to change the land on which they run, from one year to another. If turkeys are kept where they may drink from stagnant pools in barnyards, pigpens or privy vaults, sudden and fatal attacks of bowel trouble must be expected. A running stream is of great value on a turkey farm."

CHAPTER V.

SELECTION OF PARENT STOCK.

In reserving or selecting parent stock from which to raise turkeys for the market, do not overlook a most important matter, the age of the parents. Ten- or twelve-months-old turkeys are not sufficiently mature to produce the strongest progeny. Old turkeys lay larger eggs, and the young are larger and stronger when hatched. If necessity forces you to breed from stock of your own raising, keep the hens three, four, five or six years, if necessary. No judicious farmer will kill off his good heifers after they have dropped their first calves. He knows the progeny will become better and better, until age enfeebles the parent. So with turkeys. The same breeding stock may be kept, after they have proved their value, for some time. When you wish to replenish or renew the parent stock, select the best of your young hens and get a first-class tom not related to them; then you have your new stock to take the place of the others, whenever it may be deemed proper to dispose of the old ones. As Mrs. A. J. Sexson, who took the first *Farm and Home* prize for essays on turkey culture, says: "The future stock depends very much upon the parent birds, or their ancestry. Repeated breeding from inferior birds makes inferiority hereditary." When grown for exhibition purposes, pure strains only should be kept, but for marketing, cross breeds are not objectionable.

One essayist produced the best results by mating two-year-old toms to four-year-old hens. A four- or five-year-old tom is apt to attain a great weight if kept well fed,—

too heavy for the hens. Besides, if he be too fat, the eggs fail to get fertilized.

It is surprising how many attempt to raise turkeys from small and immature birds. Many who know that turkeys two years old are too young, continue to kill off the young hens for market after breeding season. As Mr. Cushman says: There seems to be a dread of having something too old or unsalable left on their hands. To breed from immature or poor specimens is to violate one of the first

FIG. 13. MR. BLOODGOOD'S FLOCK OF WHITE HOLLAND TURKEYS.

laws of breeding. Selections of the best, for generations, has given us the best and most profitable breeds of stock. The hereditary influence of such selections is of great value. The most inferior bird out of a flock of such blood may "throw back" and breed very fine stock, and do better than a much finer specimen from a poor-bred strain; but the repeated selection of inferior birds for a number of generations, makes this inferiority hereditary. The stock depends mainly on the parent birds, or their ancestry.

The most successful raisers often pay $15 to $25, including express charges, for a satisfactory gobbler. Instead of hesitating to pay the killing price for the best hen or gobbler in a flock, the turkey raiser should think himself fortunate to secure the best at three or four times the market value of the bird.

Unlike other domestic fowls, the male turkey fertilizes the eggs of an entire litter by the first copulations; the number of hens, therefore, with which he may run, may be any number from three to twenty, according to his vigor and strength.

The male bird should be proud, stately, haughty, ready to resent the presence of a stranger, yet seeming to attract attention to his plumage by the display of its beauty. His voice, as he "gobbles," should be strong and rapid. He should be always gallant to his wives, insisting that they shall admire him, and nothing and nobody else, as doubtless they do.

The female turkey should be of modest demeanor, yet with a quick, alert, bright eye; ready to respond to the gentle ministrations of the good woman who has charge of the flock; solicitous for the welfare of her young; willing and able to roost high in some tree near the house, where the proprietor may think them safe from thieves; she should have a soft flute-like voice, as she utters her peculiar cry, that so charms her lordly master; these qualities, combined with a graceful form and carriage, as she quietly and gently moves about foraging for food, make her an object of interest to every one.

No wonder that the raising of turkeys had such fascination for many people. Lords and ladies of high degree in Europe; people of all ranks in life, in nearly all parts of the world, engage in this charming pursuit; some for pastime, more for what money the work brings them; but all with an enthusiastic love for the beautiful birds. Even in Rhode Island it is customary to kill off and market the largest birds, and to breed from late turkeys and small gobblers. This inevitably decreases the size, and runs out the stock. There is a constant temptation to get the largest amount of money possible from the flocks in one season, but the returns are less in the long run. Save the best for breeders. Some experts change

FIG. 14. A MISSOURI PRIZE-WINNING BRONZE.

A portrait by Sewell for *Farm Poultry*, of the first-prize bird at the Mid-Continental (St. Louis) show. On this bird "was a plumage with a luster like burnished copper; with saddle tips almost pure white, on a body with lines truly thoroughbred, and as a thirty-six pound yearling was a most shapely Bronze gobbler. He carried a deep, round breast, and thick thighs; heavily meated, with fine-grained flesh. He was a quick-maturing tom of twenty-eight pounds at six months and two weeks of age."

gobblers every season, or every other season, but they either test the gobbler as a breeder, or know how his progeny have turned out before they depend upon him. It is best to have an extra gobbler to fall back on, should the lord of the flock be lost by disease or accident. Many western breeders agree that one can seldom obtain thrifty chicks from a young gobbler, and that a three-year-old is better than a two-year-old. Many successful turkey growers also maintain that to change gobblers every season, or every other season, as was suggested, is to make a mistake, but we don't think so, if you know the bird you buy. I. K. Felch maintains, that if one procured the finest gobbler that could be found, and mated him with extra-choice hens, they could be kept and bred from as long as they lived; not until the gobbler failed should another be procured, and he should be kept with the same hens. The progeny should be disposed of yearly and not bred from, unless mated with a strange gobbler. Of course, the breeding birds should not be too large, as hens weighing over twenty pounds are apt to lay soft-shelled eggs.

Mr Barber adds this note upon the Kentucky method: "For breeders, select broad-backed, full-breasted and short-legged ones of any variety you decide to raise. Twelve hens mated to one tom is the correct number, and some prefer young hens to adult ones, as they will lay more eggs, and if they are heavy-weight varieties, when incubating, they will not break so many, or mash so many of the young poults, as the old hens would do, while the old ones lay larger eggs, and will hatch from them stronger and hardier poults."

CHAPTER VI.

CARE OF BREEDING STOCK.

The unanimous testimony of the one hundred and seventy-seven turkey growers who responded to the call of the *Farm and Home* for essays on Turkey culture, is, that to have success in raising turkeys, attention must be given to the care of the breeding stock. This must begin "the fall before."

In the northern part of the United States, and the colder portions of the Middle, they should be housed in winter, though they can stand more cold than common fowls. Freedom to roam, on warm, sunny days, is requisite. In the Southern and Pacific States, and some portions of the Middle States, a shed open to the south is sufficient protection, so far as the climate is concerned; even trees or high rails would be better, if the temperature be not much below the freezing point. Some of the best turkeys I ever saw were in Central Illinois, and never knew shelter, their nightly perch the year round being the ridge pole of a small barn. But the rule to "follow nature" must not be misunderstood. Turkeys in their wild state seek the shelter of forests and thick shrubbery in cold weather; an open prairie, in zero weather, is not recommended for domestic birds.

Where but few turkeys are kept, they may be housed with other fowls, and receive the same feed and care, but are much more liable to disease. In all cases, the floor of the house should be covered six or more inches deep with forest leaves or straw litter, being renewed as often as it is badly soiled and trodden down.

Do not overfeed or starve your flock. The natural food of the turkey, in its wild state, consists of insects, worms, grass, berries and seeds. You can approximate that diet with your domesticated birds by the use of meat scraps, grain and soft feed. After fasting through a long, cold winter's night, such as we have from Maine to Idaho, the birds' crops are empty. The best breakfast then is a hot mush, made of wheat screenings, corn meal, cropped onions or other vegetable matter, as turnip tops,—which grow on the turnips in the cellar,—or mashed potatoes, all mixed with boiling water. Two or three times a week season this with cayenne or black pepper. A little salt now and then may not be objectionable, but that is less essential. Turkeys are not horned cattle, which need much salt. Here is my mixture for the birds' breakfast: One part by measure of corn meal, two parts wheat screenings, one part chopped onions (or two parts mashed boiled potatoes, or two parts raw chopped sweet apples), and one part meat scraps, mixed with boiling water to the consistency of thick dough. Let it stand, covered, until the meal is thoroughly swelled. Fifteen minutes is long enough. Feed what they can eat up clean. Don't let them surfeit themselves. Then throw a little grain broadcast over the litter on the floor, and let them scratch for it. Keep clean water in clean vessels before them all the time, also pounded crockery. No need of having an unsightly pile of broken dishes behind your barn or outhouse if you keep poultry. The avidity with which fowls devour this material is astonishing. I have found, by experience, that in the winter time it is better than gravel. Feed chopped rowen or clover occasionally. Keep crushed or granulated oyster shells before them always.

In the short days of our northern winters, not much need be fed at noon. Remember, you are not fattening your turkeys for market. Keep them too fat and the eggs are in danger of proving sterile. **Many breed-**

ing turkeys are over-fat in the spring, having been overfed, or given too fattening food. Frequently they die at this time as a result of overfeeding. The progeny of over-fat birds are less vigorous. Late-hatched hens that are growing all the time need more food; they cannot store up a surplus, and will lay earlier because they are thin. Feed the old turkey hens clover and less starchy food in the latter part of winter, and they will give better satisfaction. Throw them some grain at noon. Then just before sundown, give them all the hot whole grain they can eat. You may heat it in dripping pans in the stove oven, or put the grain into an iron kettle over the fire and fill with hot water. Let it come to a boil, or until you know every kernel is hot. Then scatter the hot grain well over the floor, and let the turkeys fill their crops, or until they cease calling for more. A long winter night of fourteen or fifteen hours is before them, during which they cannot eat, so a full crop of whole grain stands them in need. I followed this plan of feeding and always found it kept my poultry in good condition.

These directions, it will be seen by the observant turkey grower, are adapted to our northern latitudes. In the South and California the foregoing directions as to feeding are not wholly applicable. As regards cleanliness they are. Diseases are treated under their proper heading. Presuming that we have taken one flock of the "Birds of America" through the winter, we now come to another epoch, which requires even more care and watchfulness— the laying season.

CHAPTER VII.

LAYING AND HATCHING.

As the laying season approaches, we find that four hundred years of domestication have not changed the shy nature of the turkey, nor robbed her of her love of secrecy. From the middle of February to the middle of April, according to the latitude and climate, she begins to seek hiding places in which to lay her eggs. Here the watchfulness of the keeper must begin, and not cease until the young are able to take care of themselves. The essays given in this book are some of the most valuable contributions to turkey literature ever published. Being the simply told tales of varied personal experience, they are invaluable in the details they give of attention to little things.

The hen turkey begins to make that peculiar, musical, craking noise, and the tom is more assiduous in his attentions to his wives. He grows prouder and more gallant, and "gobbles" and displays the beauty of his plumage more than ever. In her wild state, the hen turkey lays her eggs on the ground, the nest being made of dried leaves. She selects dense shrubbery on a dry soil for its location. Your domesticated turkey will do the same, if allowed the chance. But the danger from foxes, skunks, weasels, minks, coyotes and other obstacles to success, compels you to assist nature a little. The saving of the eggs, to you, is an important matter. One Vermont woman writes, "As soon as I hear any of them making that peculiar craking noise, which they always do before they begin laying, I drive them into the horse barn, where I have prepared nests in the hay, with nest eggs in them. Sometimes I have to drive them in several mornings, keeping them shut in all the forenoon, but I always persevere until I conquer them. After they have laid two or three eggs, they will become attached to their nests. I like to have them finish laying and begin to set about the first of May." One man, who has great success with turkeys, encloses a large space by a high fence of wire netting, to prevent the turkeys laying and setting in the woods and fields. Nests are provided within the enclosure. During the laying season, the hen turkeys are driven within the enclosure to roost, and confined during the forenoon each day, until all have selected nests. When hatching, they and their young are more readily cared for and controlled. Humor the turkey's love for secrecy, if you prefer to have her lay out of doors, by setting laying coops for her in secluded places not far from your house and barn. Barrels, or "A" coops, with dried leaves or litter in them, will do. If she steals her nest in some bushes not far from the house, leave her alone, but remove the eggs daily, leaving a nest egg in the nest. When she has layed her litter she will rest awhile, and then lay another litter, when she should be allowed to sit. The eggs should be taken into the house and kept in a cool (not cold) place, packed in wheat bran, small end downward.

Turkey eggs require twenty-eight days for incubation. Coincide with the hen turkey's desire for secrecy, and let her sit in places hidden from the sight of men and dogs. Bottomless boxes that will shed rain, old barrels with two or three staves knocked out, "A" coops, measuring not less than three feet square at the base, placed in retired situations not far from the house, are all that are necessary for hatching purposes. If the turkeys were taught to lay in them, all the better. The nest should be upon the ground, and made of forest leaves or chopped hay. If turkeys are set in barrels laid on their sides, holes should be bored in the underside of the barrel to let out rain water, or it may hold water enough to spoil the eggs.

Carefully save the eggs of the first litter, if they are laid earlier in the season than you want to set them, and wait until the turkey has laid her second litter. Calculate your time, so that the chicks will come out in May. March or April in the South, and June first in the extreme North, are not far wrong. Presuming that the first litter was layed quite early, set these eggs under broody common hens of good sitting stock, as Brahmas, Cochins, or Plymouth Rocks. Under each hen place seven or eight turkey eggs; the turkey may cover sixteen to twenty. If the tom annoys the sitting turkeys, confine him, although he will not be likely to do that if one or more other turkeys are with him. If the season be late and cold storms with snow prevail, the incubation must take place in barns or sheds. Set all the eggs, if possible, at the same time. While common hens come off to feed and bathe every day, turkeys rarely leave their nests oftener than once in three days; some have been known to starve on their nest when danger threatened their eggs. Keep whole corn, wheat, oyster shells, clean water and a good dust bath accessible to them all the time.

In setting the common fowl and turkey, thoroughly powder them with Persian insect powder (Pyrethrum), using the little bellows made and sold for the purpose. Hold the hen by the legs while doing this, that every part of the skin and every feather may receive some of the powder. Scatter flour of sulphur well over the nest. If lice are detected before the four weeks are up, go through the same operation again, for of all enemies, hindrances and disarrangements which assail the poultry grower, no half dozen of them equal lice in power and persistency, or are so prevalent. Yet they can be conquered, subdued and exterminated. Two days before hatching, thoroughly powder the hen again, but put no sulphur on the nest. If the nest be upon the ground, no sprinkling of the eggs with tepid water will be necessary.

Remember, that while care and watchfulness are necessary, the shy nature of the turkey resents "fussing." After she has settled down to business, let her alone. She knows when she is hungry, and needs a bath, and if they be convenient to her she will not need your help.

Incubators may be used in hatching turkey eggs. but my advice is, learn the old-fashioned way first. The hatching is easy enough, but the disposition of the turkey to roam makes the rearing of it in confinement so far impossible.

CHAPTER VIII.

TRAINING TURKEYS TO SIT AT ANY TIME.

In France, turkeys are used as sitters and mothers when broody hens are scarce. In certain sections, turkey hens are mostly used as sitters, and many breeders keep from thirty to one hundred turkeys, which are employed for incubation, with occasional interruptions, the year round. The large hatching establishments, where a large number of incubators are used, employ turkey hens to do a part of the work. A French woman, who has had great success in beguiling her turkey hens to sit whenever she wants them to, gives an account of how it is done, in the English *Fanciers' Gazette.*

"To those who do not possess an incubator, turkeys are still more precious, as they generally get broody after a few days' training. It is not expensive business. The process is simple, and not beyond the reach of every purse. Secure a box long and wide enough to give the turkey her complete ease, though not high enough to allow her to stand up in it. This box must be shut by a cover, fastened by hooks, or kept down by a heavy stone. Four laths nailed together over a piece of wire, is the best cover to use; but one or two boards put over the box, with a little space left between them for air, will do quite well. A piece of canvas covers the whole, and keeps the bird in the dark. On the bottom of the box place a good bed of hay, slightly hollowed out in the center, and in this nest a few clear or china eggs. Then take the turkey gently, and give her five or six pieces of bread, soaked in red wine or brandy and water (half and half), or whisky and water, or any other liquor capable of giving a slight ' elevation;'

after which place her on the nest and cover her up. Morning and evening take her from the nest, put her under a coop, give her water, grain, a dust bath, and again bread soaked in some kind of spirit. Repeat this until you see that the turkey settles herself on the eggs and remains on them quietly without being covered up. Then you may give her good eggs and depend upon her to do her duty conscientiously.

"An important point upon which I cannot insist enough, is the necessity for looking for vermin before placing the hen on the nest, in order to prevent her being troubled by these pests and becoming restless, as such large birds are more liable than others to break eggs. A good sprinkling of Pyrethrum powder through the feathers and in the hay of the nest, is to be recommended. The first operation should take place by daylight. The turkey, being plunged from full light into complete darkness, when the effect of the wine begins to act and make her feel rather funny in the head, gets so frightened that she will remain on the eggs without moving. The contact with these, and her long tete-a-tete with them, develops her maternal instincts, and, as a rule, a few days are sufficient to provoke the brooding fever. I have known turkeys to get broody the day after they were set. I never train them more than eight or nine days, and give liberty to those who have not taken to the nest by that time. If properly managed, they will sit from six to eight weeks consecutively, without showing any trace of fatigue. Some breeders make them brood much longer, but it is cruel and dangerous, for sometimes the birds die on the eggs. When they do sit it is not necessary to feed them twice a day; take them up in the morning only, but let it be regularly.

"Not all turkeys are willing to be forced to sit; still, the restives are rare. When these birds are desired as sitting 'machines,' they ought to be carefully selected. Breeders who intend to go in for them should purchase once more, as wanted, and give them a trial; those which do not give entire satisfaction can be fattened and sent to market; they will pay for the remainder.

"Above all others, may it be animated or artificial brooders, turkeys are the first; to breed with them is not so expensive as using incubators or foster mothers, and gives much less trouble. Some of my readers will jump from their chair at reading this; I beg them to sit down again, and listen quietly to me. In the country, a flock of turkeys, be it very large, costs nothing to keep. Mine are turned out on a lawn, partly planted with wood, and they never get a handful of corn or any meal, until severe winter sets in—that is, when the snow covers the ground. All are in splendid condition. At night, they come home, their crops always full, and are shut up in a stable, where they find their ideal perch—an old wheel, fixed on a stake a few feet from the ground. In our climate, the winters are not long, and rarely very severe. We may calculate to have to feed our turkeys during two months. The manure, which they produce in great quantities the whole year round, pays amply for the expense of food during that period, which is also the time we require their services for brooding. Thus the cost of feeding ought not to be taken into account; nevertheless, if we do, the food of four turkeys, which will breed one hundred eggs, will not come to the cost of the heating of an incubator of same capacity. Such a machine will consume, per day, about one litre of petroleum of first quality, at the rate of five pence the litre. Four turkeys will not eat more than threepence worth. As for the trouble, I do not think it makes more labor to take the hens from the nests once a day than to turn, morning and evening, a quantity of eggs, clean the lamp, fill up the water, etc., without counting that the slightest neglect may expose the whole contents of the incubator. With turkeys, nothing like this is to be dreaded. Of mild and submissive disposition, they can be handled in any way, and seldom break any of the eggs entrusted to their care. They will breed with the same tenderness all sorts of eggs, be they of geese or of pheasants.

"Last year I received from England a few sittings of Bantam eggs. Having no broody hens ready, I got three in my neighborhood. At the sight of the small eggs, so different from their own, the broody hens got quite wild, and would have destroyed the lot had we not taken them away. I sent them back from where they came, and immediately began to train a few turkeys. My flock consisted of three large birds, which get broody after twenty-four hours' training. Two days later, I gave all the eggs to one of these, which brooded them without breaking a single one.

"Turkeys are very attentive mothers, and protect their chickens well. I never had one taken by vermin or birds of prey, which abound in the grounds around, because of the proximity of a forest, although my turkeys, with their young ones, are free to run where they like, and go sometimes three or four hundred yards from the house. If they know each other, several may be allowed to run together without danger of fighting. These goodies will accept any change or addition of chickens, and brood the newcomers as tenderly as their own. I often saw turkeys, whose chicks had been joined to others, adopt large chickens more than two months old, which had been forsaken by the hen.

"Training turkeys to force them to sit does not take away their laying qualities, when they are properly managed. Therefore, allow them to lay their batch of eggs after they have brooded and raised your early chickens. They will ask to sit immediately they have finished laying; you may let them, and have no fear of overworking.

"And now, if my readers will believe in one who speaks by experience, and not upon hearsay, they will give my favorite brooding machines a trial, and admit afterwards that we French people do not always tell boastful stories or propagate hoaxes."

Doubtless many would be opposed to giving whisky or any spirits to poultry for any purpose, and this may not be necessary, even to insure success. Mr W. E. Stevenson, of Arkansas, writes the *Reliable Poultry Journal* that he trains his turkeys to sit at any time, and succeeds without administering either corn or grape juice. He treats his turkeys kindly, so as to have them very tame, and uses hens that are from three to ten years old. In the winter, when he wants to set them, he makes a nest in a barrel or box of suitable size, then warms six to ten china eggs and puts them in the nest, and puts the turkey on them. This is done in the evening, or when it is growing dark. A sack or quilt is hung over the opening, to darken the nest. He feeds very lightly for three days. By the third day he can tell whether the turkey has become broody. If she has, from twenty to thirty eggs are given her, according to her size. Turkeys, under proper care, can be depended upon to keep to their nests for ten weeks, but for best results should not be made to do this work over six weeks. Mr Stevenson thus successfully sets his turkeys at any time, without violating his Prohibition principles.

Mr. Samuel Cushman says, from his own experience, that turkeys can be made to sit whenever required. A young turkey hen that never laid an egg was shut on a nest of china eggs, and there was no trouble in getting her to settle down. The first two times she was put off to feed, she was caught and placed on the nest and shut in, but after that the nest was left uncovered and she came off when whenever she chose. We never found her off the nest. The shed in which she was set had a slat front, so she was confined and could not go out of sight of the nest or get away. This turkey was not a tame one, by any means. We can control our turkeys better if set within a large building

TRAINING TURKEYS TO SIT AT ANY TIME.

or enclosure. Turkeys can be used to hatch the eggs of hens, ducks and geese, and the raiser who does not have an artificial hatcher will not have to delay operations until hens get ready to set, or until he can secure the desired number.

CHAPTER IX.

REARING THE TURKEY CHICKS.

The turkey chicks having been hatched, they will require the breeder's utmost and constant attention for the first eight or ten weeks, for on the management of the chicks depends the success or failure of turkey rearing. Turkeys, when chicks, being exceeding delicate (the most delicate of any domesticated poultry), and liable to be not only decimated, but entire broods exterminated by a sudden cold wind or a slight shower, and requiring, as they do, feeding every two hours, or six times a day, it is advisable for those who are unable to spare the time to give the necessary attention, not to attempt breeding turkeys, for they will only meet with severe losses and disappointment.

The chicks, having broken the shells by themselves, without any fussy interference by the owner, may be left to themselves for twenty-four hours, though the shells may be removed and something placed in front of the nest, if it be made in a box, to prevent any of the chicks falling out and getting cold. The chicks having, just previously to emerging from the shell, drawn into their body the yolk, they are sufficiently sustained for twenty or twenty-four hours or so, and require no feeding until the following day. If the day be warm and fine, they may be placed outdoors, in a dry situation; if cold and damp, or windy, they are better kept under cover, though not in a close atmosphere, but where there is plenty of ventilation, a large open shed protected from the wind being the best. A warm bed having been provided, made of chaff, dry sawdust or dry horse droppings, all over a bed of dry sand and coal ashes, to prevent damp arising, place the coop, which should be previously lime-washed, over it, facing south, and the mother and chicks inside. The poults hatched under common hens should be given the mother turkey in the night. Some breeders prefer bottoms to the coops, but unless the ground be very damp, that is not necessary. If you dusted the mother with insect powder two days before hatching, there will be no lice to annoy them.

On the second day the chicks may receive their first meal. On one point all turkey growers agree: no "sloppy" food must be given the young birds. In a natural state, turkey chicks feed largely upon flies, spiders, grasshoppers, grubs, snails, slugs, worms, ant eggs, etc., and if watched on a bright day will be seen to be constantly chasing flies, etc., about the meadows and woods. Berries, seeds, etc., make the variation. The first meal should be hard-boiled eggs (boiled twenty minutes), and stale wheat bread dipped in hot milk, the milk squeezed out, and both crumbled fine and seasoned with black pepper. This feed may be continued for two or three weeks, with now and then a variation to thick clabbered milk, or Dutch cheese in place of the egg. Let it be known that the egg is a substitute for insects, which the young turkey has in its wild state; so, as opportunities open for the chicks to get insects, the egg should be omitted. Dry meal must not be given

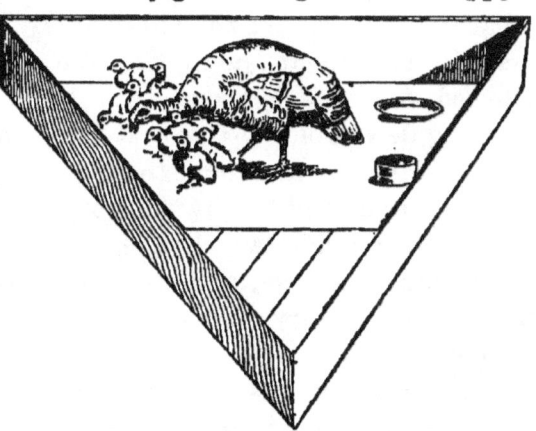

FIG. 15. PEN TO CONFINE LITTLE TURKEYS, UNTIL OLD ENOUGH TO JUMP OVER; MOTHER AT LIBERTY.

them, not wet meal insufficiently swelled. If the meal swells in their crops, death is almost certain. The best way to feed Indian meal is in the form of corn bread or "Johnny cake." After the young birds are three weeks old, omit the eggs and give meat scraps and ground bone. Clean water or milk must be before them all the time. For runs, the best are three fourteen-inch boards set on edge so as to form a triangle, with the coop in one corner, or shorter boards over one corner, for shelter from the sun by day and dews by night. Every day or two, move two of these boards so as to form another triangle, Fig. 15, adjacent to the site of the old one. By the time the chicks are old enough to jump·over the boards, they may be allowed to wander about with their mother, after the morning dew is off. After that time, three feedings a day are sufficient, and when they are weaned, feeding at morning and night only is enough. With a good range over wheat stubble, which they can have in the Western States and territories, and plenty of grasshoppers, no other feeding is necessary after they are educated to come home to roost.

Mr Barber writes: " Our turkeys lay and sit in large roomy coops, two and one-half feet long by two feet wide, two feet high in front, with a slope of six inches to the rear; we keep the turkey hens, with their broods, in a lot, on short grass."

Instead of cooping brooding turkeys to prevent them from roaming too much, W. P. Lewis, who raises 90 per cent of his hatch, fastens the hen with a cord to a peg in the ground, after the manner cows are tied out to pasture. After being pegged down for a few days, the hens are "shingled" so they cannot fly over walls and fences, and are then allowed free range. In "shingling," or "boarding," turkeys, a thin board or shingle, in which holes are bored, is· fastened across the shoulders of the bird by soft cords, tape or strips of cloth. When of the proper shape and the boards are in the right place, and the cords are not tied too tightly, they may be worn twelve months without injury to the turkey. By this method the birds may be confined to one field as easily as sheep. This is better and surer than clipping one wing. The only objection to it is that turkeys thus hampered are almost at the mercy of dogs. When the board is first adjusted, the turkeys try to free themselves, but they usually accept the situation in less than an hour, and do not seem to mind them afterward. Various other boards are used, Fig. 16 giving the Rhode Island pattern, and Fig 17 the Western style. The strings are usually tied on the top of the board. In fastening the Western style of board, the string is passed down from one hole in front of the wing, close to the body, and

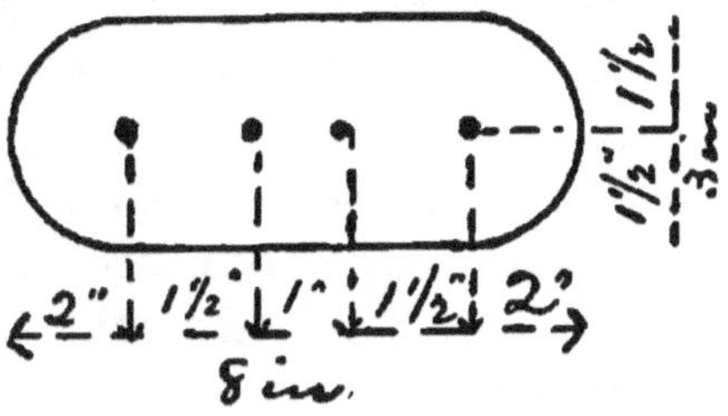

FIG. 16. RHODE ISLAND TURKEY SHINGLE.

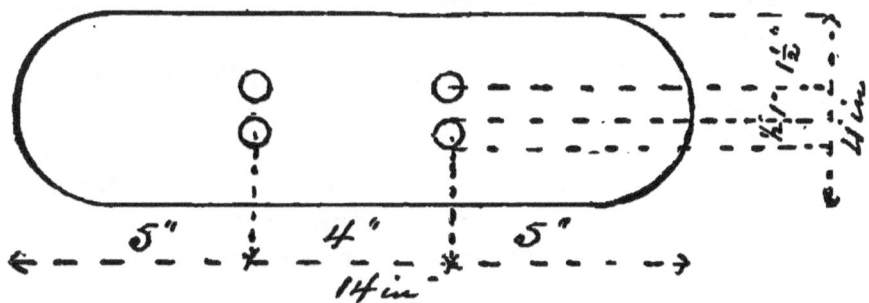

FIG. 17. WESTERN STYLE OF TURKEY SHINGLE.

around under the wing and up through the other hole, and is tied on top of the board. An ordinary shingle is strong enough for most hens, but large gobblers require something stronger, and light barrel staves are often used; a three-eighths-inch auger hole is then necessary, but usually a gimlet is sufficient.

The young chicks must have green food. If they cannot obtain plenty of grass, give chopped lettuce, dandelions, onion tops (these last sparingly), turnip tops, e c. Buckwheat, cracked corn, and wheat may be given at night, after they get large enough. Do not leave food around. Feed each time only so much as will be eaten up clean. After the first two weeks give sour milk freely. After they can get insects, no other meat than the milk will be necessary. The particular enemies of the young turkeys are lice and diarrhœa, but both may be conquered. These will be treated in the chapter on Hindrances.

During the feathering period, the chicks must have plenty of bone- and feather-forming material. This is supplied best in the form of finely chopped meat and green bones. A good bone mill or cutter is indispensable when much poultry are kept. See that they have grit, in the form of pounded crockery, oyster shells and clean gravel. The best thing I ever used was small sea shells from the sea coast of Connecticut. They cost about a dollar per barrel.

In addition to the foregoing, the following hints brought out by the most careful inquiry by the Rhode Island Experiment Station, of the methods pursued by the best turkey specialists in that State, are of interest: Little turkeys do best if kept and fed separate from fowls and chickens. They are weak and tender creatures, and as they grow very fast, require an abundance of nutritive and easily digested food, but it must not be too concentrated. Too rich food, too much food that is hard to digest, or a lack of green food, will cause bowel trouble. Little turkeys require food oftener than little chickens. Feed little and often. Give cooked food until they grow enough to develop the red about the head, or green food, like chopped onions and lettuce, if they are confined to a pen. Remember that little chickens thrive under confinement that would cause disease and death among little turkeys. If the little turkeys are cooped, remove them to fresh, dry ground frequently. Dampness, lice and filth make short work of them. Give them their food on clean surfaces.

Young turkeys should not be out in heavy showers until their backs are well covered with feathers. If they get wet, they may die from chill, unless put in a warm room to dry. Black and red pepper and ginger in the food or drinking water aid them to overcome a chill, and are of great value on cold or damp days, and are a preventive

FIG. 18. COOP FOR BROODING TURKEY, WHILE THE CHICKS ARE AT LIBERTY.

of bowel trouble in both old and young turkeys. Some find that young turkeys do best when neither they nor the hen is confined, providing they are put in a pasture lot, high and dry, where the grass is short and there are no trees. No more than three litters are cooped in a five-acre lot.

Rhode Island turkey growers are careful to use only Northern corn, at least a year old, in feeding both little turkeys and grown ones, as new corn is apt to cause diarrhœa. Messrs Browning & Chappell, an illustration of one of whose flocks is given in Fig. 21, use corn bread, as suggested in this chapter, but in making this bread the meal is mixed with sweet milk, and is given time to swell, and is then baked. After a few weeks, a portion of scalded cracked corn is mixed with the crumbs, and the proportion is gradually increased until clear scalded cracked corn is given.

FIG. 19. SHED FOR SHELTERING LITTLE TURKEYS AT NIGHT.

They consider it very important that the cracked corn be always well scalded and allowed to swell before feeding. On cold or stormy days a small quantity of black pepper is added to the bread crumbs or cracked corn. They find that turkeys that forage on green oats will have diarrhœa.

At the Rhode Island Station it was found that confining the little turkeys at night prevents their being entangled and lost in the long, wet grass, but it is detrimental to their welfare and should not be continued too long. If possible, they should have full liberty where the

FIG. 20. SHED FOR SHELTERING LITTLE TURKEYS AT NIGHT.

grass is short. Their nature is such that they need cold air and a great deal of exercise. Restriction of liberty, with light feeding, soon puts them out of condition; while full feeding, even with liberty, prevents their taking full exercise, and causes disease of the digestive organs, and they are lost or do not thrive.

If the young birds have done well at six or **eight weeks,** they begin to "throw the red," as it is **termed,** viz: to develop the red carunculous formation about the head and neck, so characteristic of the turkey. If the turkey chicks be late hatched or weakly, it is retarded sometimes another month. Should the growth, from whatever cause, be checked when young, they will never make large and vigorous birds. After they have "thrown the red," the sexes can be distinguished, and they are then termed poults. They should not be allowed to perch too early, but bedded down upon chaff, leaves, etc., or they will have crooked breasts. Later on, the fleshy appendage over the beak, and the billy or horsehair-like tuft on the breast, make their appearance in the male birds, which, with tail erected and outspread, and with the whole body inflated with pomp, can be easily distinguished from their more somber sisters. At the time of "throwing the red," the young turkeys pass through their chicken molt, another critical period in their life. The birds lose their appetite and languish several days. They require now more stimulating food and a larger meat diet. Being insectivorous, the best range young turkeys can have is among shrubbery, bushes and such like. If the weather be open and fine, and the birds have a little extra care for a short time, they become as hardy, as adults, as they were delicate when young.

In Kentucky, writes Mr Barber, the young should be fed for the first week on corn bread in which there is plenty of egg, and stale light bread soaked in milk. With the range of a blue-grass woodland, and plenty of insects, the poults grow very rapidly; when they are six to eight weeks of age they are permitted to roost in trees.

CHAPTER X.

FATTENING AND MARKETING—FEATHERS.

After the first of October, especially if frosts have lessened the supply of insects and other food which they have gathered themselves, begin issuing extra rations to your turkeys. This is to keep them in good growing condition until the fattening begins, which should be three or four weeks before Thanksgiving. For breakfast, feed boiled potatoes, carrots, sweet apples, etc., mixed with bran and corn meal, seasoned with black pepper once or twice a week, and twice a week add pulverized charcoal to the food. At night give whole grain. Keep pure water or milk in convenient vessels for drink.

Three weeks before Thanksgiving, separate from the rest of the flock all that you design for the Thanksgiving market. This separation is necessary, because it is not desirable to fatten those which are to be kept over for breeding stock, or the late-hatched ones that are not yet large enough for market. Feeding the whole flock extra rations of fattening food is not only a waste of food, but works injury to all which are not soon to be killed.

But do not confine the flock to be fattened in small pens; remember, the nature of the birds requires liberty; rather confine those which you wish to keep over. Turkeys having full liberty will devour much food and take on fat rapidly. Fattening turkeys will not wander so much, as after being put on full feed they will be more content to remain nearer home.

Give the fattening turkeys all they can eat four times a day, from the time when you commence full feeding until twenty-four hours before slaughtering time. The first three of the daily meals should be of cooked potatoes and corn meal, or of corn meal scalded with milk or water, and the last of whole corn, varied with wheat or buckwheat. Always use corn a year old; new corn causes much trouble and may kill them. Give the first meal as soon as possible after daylight, and the last just before dark. Feed each time all they will eat up clean, but leave no food by them. Feed the pounded charcoal occasionally, and keep a supply of gravel where they can help themselves. Twenty days of such feeding will put turkeys that have been growing and in good health, in the best possible condition for market. In Rhode Island, turkeys are not fed much in September and October, but in November they get all the whole old corn they will eat, but are kept away from barns and buildings.

TURKEY BROILERS FOR FANCY PROFITS.

Turkey raisers who are located near summer resorts where the wealthy congregate, can probably make a market for turkey broilers. At places like Newport, and similar resorts, there is a demand for such birds in July and August. They may be sold when they weigh from one and one-half to four pounds each, and bring from $1.75 to $2.25 each. They are generally sold by the price or pair, instead of by the pound.

Near by raisers can control this trade, because turkeys at this age cannot be shipped long distances. If dressed, they are so lean and tender that they do not keep well. If placed on ice, they become discolored in a very short time.

Where more young turkeys are raised than can be brought to maturity without overstocking the place, it will be wise to seek such a market for the surplus, or for all of them, where disease is almost sure to kill them off after they become larger.

CATCHING TURKEYS IN THE FALL.

Beginners, especially, have much difficulty in securing their turkeys when they desire to kill and market them. A bungling and unsuccessful attempt to catch a flock may make them so suspicious that they cannot be surrounded or approached the remainder of the season. Repeated attempts to catch them increases their wildness, and fre-

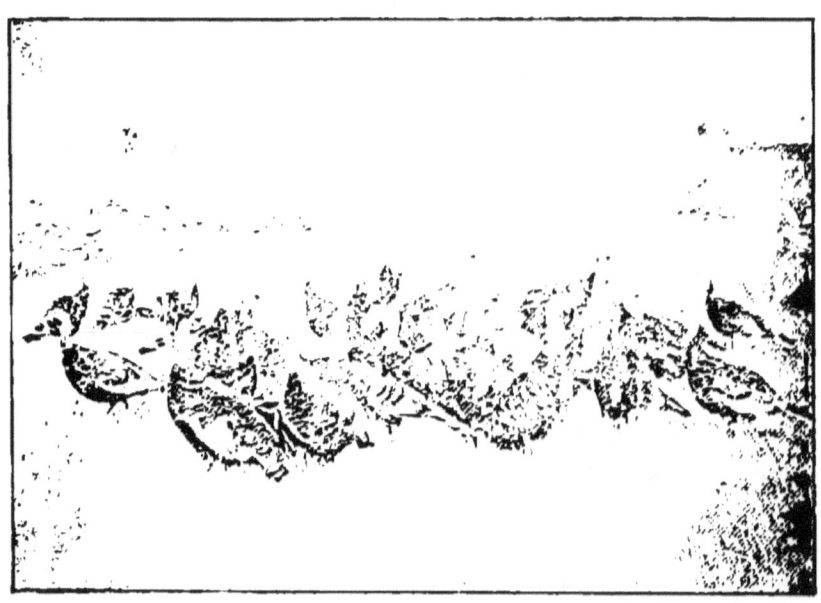

FIG. 21. FROM A PHOTOGRAPH OF BROWNING & CHAPPELL'S FLOCK, RHODE ISLAND.

quently the only way to secure them has been to shoot them. This is more apt to be the case if the stock contains wild blood. Old hands at the business have learned by experience the proper course to pursue. The usual plan is to get the birds into a barn or carriage shed and shut them in. In order to do this they are fed for a long time in front of or just within the place in which they are to be caught. Later, the feed is placed within the building, and they become so familiar with it that they are unsuspicious when within. The feeder takes pains not to appear to notice or watch them, and moves about very slowly and quietly. When they are to be caught, the doors of the building are suddenly closed, or a covered yard of wire netting is built in front of the building and closed when all are in. Usually when they find they are confined, they become frightened, and fly back and forth, or huddle up in corners, and sometimes many are smothered beneath the pile of frightened birds. In flying back and forth against the netting, their wings become bruised, and their appearance when dressed is injured.

To overcome this drawback, certain raisers have improved the usual makeshift catching place by building a long, low, dark pen back of the barn or shed. This pen extends alongside of the building, and is at right angles with the entrance to it, and at the extreme end is about two feet high. Up to the time of their being caught, the end is left open and the birds frequently find their way through it. When closely approached from the front, when feeding in the building, they rely upon this means of escape and are not frightened. When they are to be caught, only what the pen will comfortably take, are driven in. They do not discover that the end is closed until it is too late to try to turn back. The turkeys that are not to be caught are first driven away, otherwise they may be alarmed and become unmanageable. No turkey that is thus caught and has learned the mysteries of the trap, is ever allowed to escape, or its suspicions would be communicated to the others. When shut in this pen they are quiet, and when a man goes to catch them there is no struggle; he simply reaches out and takes them by the legs. The pen is too dark and narrow for them to fly, and too low for them to crowd one upon another.

KILLING AND PICKING.

Poultry shrinks about one-third in dressing. If you make your own prices, bear this proportion in mind. Live turkey at twelve cents a pound is nearly the same as sixteen cents dressed, not reckoning the cost of labor in dressing. If you market your turkeys where you get eighteen cents dressed, you cannot afford to sell them alive for less than thirteen and one-half cents a pound, unless you deduct cost of dressing, which is worth about eight cents per head.

Deprive the birds of food and drink for twelve hours previous to killing. This length of time is sufficient to empty the crop, which is necessary to have the dressed turkey keep well. If starved for more than twelve hours, the birds begin to pine, or shrink in flesh, giving them more or less of a woody appearance. The length of time they are confined without food beyond twelve hours, will affect the appearance of the stock. Kill by bleeding in the mouth or neck, and pick clean, but do not attempt to stick poultry in the mouth unless you understand it, because, if not properly done, they will only half "bleed out," and when being picked, the blood will follow every feather, giving the bird a bad appearance, and rendering it almost unsalable. Never stun them by knocking on the head or pounding on the back, as it causes the blood to settle, and injures the sale of the stock. If you sell the birds with the heads removed, kill them by beheading, leavnig the neck as long as possible.

Have two stout cords hang from a joist or horizontal pole overhead, with a loop in the lower end of each. Place a loop over each foot of the turkey, and have the body hang at a convenient hight for you to pick, standing. After killing, hang the body quickly, and remove the feathers before the body gets cold; pull out tail and wing feathers clean. Practice will soon perfect you in this, so that you will have all done, the intestines drawn and all, while there is yet heat in the body.

For the Boston market it is fully as well to leave head on and entrails in, on all turkeys up to the regular Thanksgiving shipments, but no turkeys should ever be scalded for this market. Never remove liver, heart or gizzard. For the New York, Philadelphia and Chicago markets, turkeys should never, at any time or at any season, be drawn or headed, and scalded stock will sometimes sell fully as well in those markets as dry picked.

PACKING AND SHIPPING.

In packing turkeys, assort them carefully, putting the large ones, also the small ones and any old bulls, each by

Turkey Boxes 14 x 22 x 26

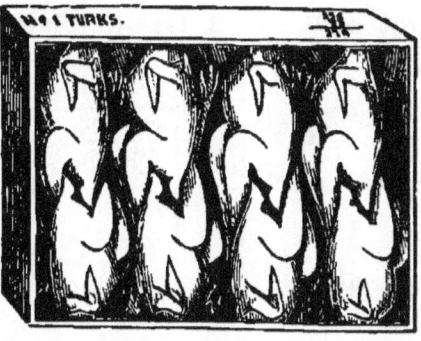

Chicken Boxes 8 x 16 x 22

FIG. 22. TURKEYS PACKED FOR MARKET.

themselves, and mark the number of turkeys in the package. During Thanksgiving week, large fancy turkeys, weighing from twelve to fifteen pounds each, generally command the best prices of the year. The market is then usually filled with "fair to poor" stock, which goes at low figures; but even ten-pound turkeys, fat and well dressed, bring good prices, unless, as is sometimes the case, warm, rainy weather demoralizes the market. Make your packages as uniform as possible. Nice boxes of regular dimensions are much better than irregular ones. We subjoin a cut giving best sizes used for turkeys and chickens, and showing style of packing generally preferred by our customers.

Western shippers who send large quantities had better adopt these packages and style of packing, even if at considerable trouble and expense, as it will give them a decided advantage over other shippers who use old boxes of all sizes, ready to fall apart on arrival—because, when shipped as above suggested, it insures quick sales, prompt returns and highest market prices for quality of stock.

During cold weather, poultry can be shipped any day in the week, either by express or freight. It should be entirely cold, but not frozen, before being packed. Boxes are the best packages. Line them with paper and pack so closely that the contents cannot move, but never use straw, and never wrap dressed poultry in paper. On the cover, distinctly mark the kind and quality of contents—the gross weight and correct tare in plain figures, thus:

```
20 No. 1          250
Turks.             40
                  ---
                  210

   ADDRESS OF COMMISSION
         MERCHANT.
```

```
Choice            125
Chicks.            20
                  ---
                  105

   ADDRESS OF COMMISSION
         MERCHANT.
```

Also the merchant's name and that of the shipper, unless he is known by the number of his stencil. Stencils are furnished free for this purpose, when desired. When the correct tare of a package is omitted, the entire contents have to be removed to ascertain the weight of the poultry, and if frozen, it is often impossible to do this without tearing the package to pieces, and if not frozen, it causes much extra work and delay, which will sometimes prevent the sale, especially if the customer is in a hurry, as is usually the case in the busy poultry season. All these little points should be closely observed by turkey raisers and shippers, for they all count in selling turkeys to the best advantage and at the least expense.

BEST TIME TO SELL.

The greatest market for dressed turkeys is Boston, but it is more particular than Western and Southern market centers. Yet the best goods sold at the right time will always command the best prices in any market. W. H. Rudd, Son & Co., one of the largest concerns in the turkey and poultry commission business, in addition to the above directions for packing and shipping, write:

In years past few shipments of turkeys were received on this market previous to Thanksgiving, but it has been the aim of producers and shippers to make earlier shipments each year, until at present we can say our season for young, small turkeys ("chicken turkeys," so called) opens in September. Some lots, in the vicinity of Newport and other celebrated shore resorts, are offered as chicken turkeys to broil, as early as August; but the general market is not supplied until the middle of September. There is, at this time, a very limited demand for a few small turkeys to broil, but the market is overstocked with this grade after a few shipments have arrived, and shippers are advised to send none dressing under eight pounds each. The majority of early shipments are from Indiana, Southern Illinois and Ohio, and the market generally opens at twenty to twenty-five cents per pound, but is dependent, in a few days, on the supply and demand, an oversupply sometimes forcing the market, in October, to very low figures. Shipments from Vermont and New Hampshire, the early part of October, have for the last few years held quite steady at twenty cents for large nine- or ten-pound turkeys, and as at this time they need not be drawn or headed, it is quite profitable to the raiser to make early shipments. Stock, at this season, should be ice packed, and the bulk from Western points are packed in barrels.

The early part of November, Kentucky commences shipments to our market, and the quality of stock from this State has shown a great improvement in the past three years. Stock from there is generally headed and packed dry in boxes and shipped by express, and for some years we have seen but few lots at this time that have not come through in good condition. It is question whether it is necessary or not, to draw and head any turkeys before the regular Thanksgiving shipments, as up to that time we think all lots will bring fully as much not drawn or headed.

Boston, at Thanksgiving time, is the distributing point for all cities and large towns in New England; the bulk of shipments first arrive here, and the number of turkeys disposed of five days previous to that time is enormous, some

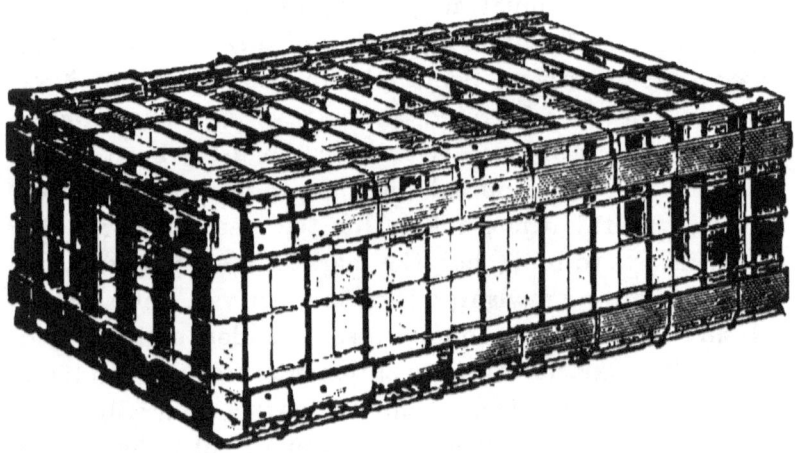

FIG. 23. OPEN CRATE FOR SHIPPING DRESSED TURKEYS IN COOL WEATHER.

of the large commission houses sometimes selling $10,000 to $12,000 worth the Monday previous. Shipments intended for this trade should always be timed to arrive here not later than Saturday or Monday previous, and some shippers have found it advantageous to get their stock here one or two days earlier. There is a special poultry train through parts of Vermont and New Hampshire, which lands their shipments the Saturday afternoon previous to Thanksgiving, and raisers should arrange to get all their large-sized turkeys here for Thanksgiving, as they are wanted at that time as large as possible, while later in the season smaller sizes command a premium. After Christmas, stock weighing over twelve pounds each are hard sellers, but for the Thanksgiving trade there is a demand for as large stock as can be produced, and for some years past extra large fancy stock from New England points has ranged in price from eighteen to twenty cents, the latter quotation being extreme, and only for exceptionally fine stock. Fourteen cents has been a fair average for fine Western stock, the range being twelve to sixteen cents, with No. 2 stock ten cents or under. But few lots of turkeys from the New England States are received here after Thanksgiving, everything of suitable size generally having been rushed in at that time, and from then until shipments cease in February or the early part of March, the supply is dependent on the Western States.

At Christmas there is some demand for large turkeys, but medium sizes are called for, the prices at this time ranging from twelve to fourteen cents for stock of good quality. Dealers buying to place in cold storage for the spring and summer trade, take advantage of any unusually low prices at this time, but the general bulk of cold storage stock is placed through January and February, and usually at prices ranging from eleven to thirteen cents. The regular shipments from the West are generally cleaned up by the last of February, and stock arriving after this date is much below cold storage stock, as regards quality; that stored being depended on for best trade until the new crop begins to move again, in September and October. There are, of course, regular shipments through the spring and summer months, of fresh-killed ice-packed turkeys, old hens and toms, but such stock is about the same quality as fowl and old cocks, and the range in price is wide, from eight to eleven cents per pound.

There are not enough turkeys' eggs arriving on this market at any season of the year to establish quotations.

Late in the season a few are received from the West and North, mixed in with hens' eggs, and which sell at the same price.

TURKEY FEATHERS.

There is some profit in saving and marketing turkey feathers, but this depends largely upon circumstances. The choicest tail feathers are worth more than any other kind, and are put to various uses. An industry which has grown to considerable proportions in the last few years is the manufacture of feather dusters from turkey tail feathers. These, to a certain extent, replace ostrich feather dusters, which are so expensive as to put them out of the reach of very many people. Carefully selected turkey tail feathers are freed from imperfections, and so much of the quill split away that the "backbone" of the feather is elastic, yet strong. These are grouped, and bound and finished into a very serviceable duster. A few of the wing feathers are used in this way. Another use of certain choice feathers is in making featherbone, entering into dress stays. At certain seasons and in certain years, there is a considerable demand for white turkey feathers for use in the millinery trade, decking the bonnet of a fashionable woman, who rests content in the belief that she is wearing a Parisian headdress made perfect by ostrich feathers from South Africa. A certain class of trade handles only body feathers, having no use for those with stiff quills. Choice body feathers are very much used for cheap pillows and for mattresses; they must, however, be treated by a process which makes them soft and fluffy, and the prices paid for the feathers in the raw state are usually so low as to prevent much profit in the handling of them.

The most favorable time to market turkey feathers is late in the fall and during the winter and early spring months. Then there is a larger demand, and established market prices at all leading cities, while during the summer the inquiry is irregular and quotations often purely nominal. To command any sort of attention in the market, the feathers should be dry-picked after the turkey is killed and before being scalded. Scalded turkey feathers are shown very little favor in any market and are often quite unsalable. They are frequently received in the big markets in such poor shape that they are sent to the dump.

The best way to ship feathers is in crates or light boxes. They should be sorted, tail, wing and pointers. The latter are used only in making corsets, and can be packed in any style, a good way being in muslin sacks. The wings and tail feathers should be handled carefully and kept clean. The tail feathers should be free from body feathers in order to bring top prices. Shippers sometimes send wing, tail and pointers, without sorting. While they will sell this way, the price is based on an allowance for the cost of separating and repacking. The feathers should be laid straight and packed tightly. Shoe or hat boxes are well suited for this, or light cases made of laths will be found strong enough, and still afford a saving in freight or express charges. A point to be remembered is that the feathers must not be jammed and packed crosswise, but should appear regularly placed when the box or crate is opened.

Unless large numbers of turkeys are slaughtered, it may not pay to ship the feathers. But when one dresses the turkeys of an entire neighborhood, it might be well to sort the feathers and find a market for them. At times, a demand exists for pure white wing and tail feathers, at a slight premium over colored feathers. The proportion of white feathers, clean and perfect, is so small, however, as to scarcely pay for the time and labor of sorting. To command top prices they must be sorted clean of all short feathers. This is a slow and laborious undertaking to any but an expert feather sorter, and if such is employed especially for the purpose, the added cost frequently equals the net value of the feathers after deducting freight, cartage and commission charges. The subjoined table represents recent quotations in Chicago, and the price at St. Louis and other leading markets is much the same, freight differences considered. The rate of freight from interior shipping points can be readily learned, remembering that the railroad company charges for one hundred pounds for any single package weighing less than that.

Turkey tail, choice and clear, per pound,	15 and 25 cents
Turkey tail, mixed with skirt feathers,	12 and 18 cents
Turkey wing, from first two joints,	8 and 12 cents
Turkey wing, tail and pointers,	6 and 12 cents
Turkey wing and tail, clear,	10 and 15 cents
Turkey wing and pointers,	5 and 8 cents
Turkey pointers,	3 and 4 cents
Turkey body, dry and choice,	2 and 3 cents

CHAPTER XI.

SHELTER—MARKING.

As mentioned before, much housing of turkeys is not needed. Health, vigor and strength of constitution, both in the parent and young stock, are the all-important considerations. High roosts, if they perch out of doors, are necessary, that foxes, etc, do not get them. Large fence rails set horizontally on uprights, ten or twelve feet from the ground, are the next best things to the large limbs of trees. In the more northern latitudes the housing need not begin until snow falls. The birds' should always roost near the house or barn, that they may be kept tame.

There is more danger that turkeys will be kept in too warm houses, than in too cold. A tight house with draughts from a ventilator, such as is used with common hens, would be too confining for turkeys. The healthy adult can stand almost any amount of cold, rain or snow, but must have cold, pure air, and a dry place to roost and to stay in when he feels like it. Observe the nature of wild turkeys in this respect. A windbreak is highly desirable, but a house is not the thing for old turkeys unless it is the size of a barn and built as open.

At the Rhode Island Station, although the turkey house was airy and high, the young turkeys which were allowed to roost therein did not thrive. The slat door was open after dark, that they might leave in the morning as early as they chose, but they seemed to be affected unfavorably. Those allowed full liberty and outdoor roosts were much more thrifty. During the winter it was the same with the old turkeys that roosted in the house. Young and old were out of condition and had colds, with swelled faces, while those in the trees seemed bright and healthy. The contrast was so great that in midwinter, during the coldest weather, those roosting in the building were shut out and compelled to roost in the trees, and in a few days they had improved and many of them were as well as ever. The shed was kept perfectly clean and they were not overcrowded. Satisfactory results may be obtained in winter if the roosts are placed in the center of an old, empty hay barn, with quarter-inch cracks between the boards on all sides. The less housing turkeys have, except as described for young turkeys, the better.

When turkeys are confined, a dust bath is indispensable. Take two boards, each four or five feet long, set them on edge in one corner of your house, where there is good light, so as to form a square, and fill it with dry loam in late summer or early fall. Sifted coal ashes may be used to mix with the loam, but wood ashes should not, unless they first be leached; even then, they will prove of more value to you on your garden soil. Never, in any case, allow wood ashes to mix with poultry manure. The alkali of the ashes liberates the ammonia of the manure, and besides the dreadful odor which arises, you lose much of the fertilizing properties of the manure.

TURKEY SHEDS.

Turkey sheds are for housing young turkeys in stormy or boisterous weather. Almost always in May we have, in the Northern States, a cold rain storm, lasting from three to nine days, that will kill more turkey chicks, unless they are guarded from exposure to the rain, than the ax will kill at the next Thanksgiving. When the farmer's wife has but two or three broods of young turkeys, she can move them into dry coops in the barn, woodshed, or any place where they can be kept dry, until pleasant weather returns, but the turkey grower who intends to grow 200 to 500 or 1000 turkeys will find turkey sheds necessary. Properly constructed and judiciously used, they will save their entire cost in one or two seasons.

Build them any convenient length, twenty or more feet. Let the width be ten feet at the bottom, roof ten feet, with a receding front seven and one-half feet high, and four and one-half feet high in the rear. Have the roof boards project a little in front, and six or eight inches at the rear. It can be made of rough boards battened, and the roof covered with Standard roofing paper. Keep the mother hens in coops in the back part of the shed, and give the little turkeys the freedom of the floor. On pleasant days, after the dew is off, open the doors and give all liberty until night, but on rainy days keep the broods shut in. Move the coops often and rake the sand. In a shed like this, say twenty feet long, you can shelter one hundred to one hundred and twenty-five young turkeys easily, until they are grown of sufficient size and age to be out at all times in all weathers.

Sheds for sheltering broods of little turkeys at night may be made, as shown in Figs. 19 and 20. These are six feet long, three feet wide, three feet high in front, and two feet at rear. Of course they may be made higher and wider. Slats are best for front, if sheds are large, as there is less danger of injury to turkeys by flying against them.

MARKING TURKEYS FOR IDENTIFICATION.

SAMUEL CUSHMAN.

As previously stated, turkeys do not thrive unless allowed free range. If enclosed in a large park by woven wire fence, or kept on an island, they can be controlled, but when given full liberty they roam over adjoining farms. In a neighborhood where many keep them, the different flocks are liable to meet, run together and get pretty well mixed. If not separated immediately, they may roost together, and roam as one flock the rest of the

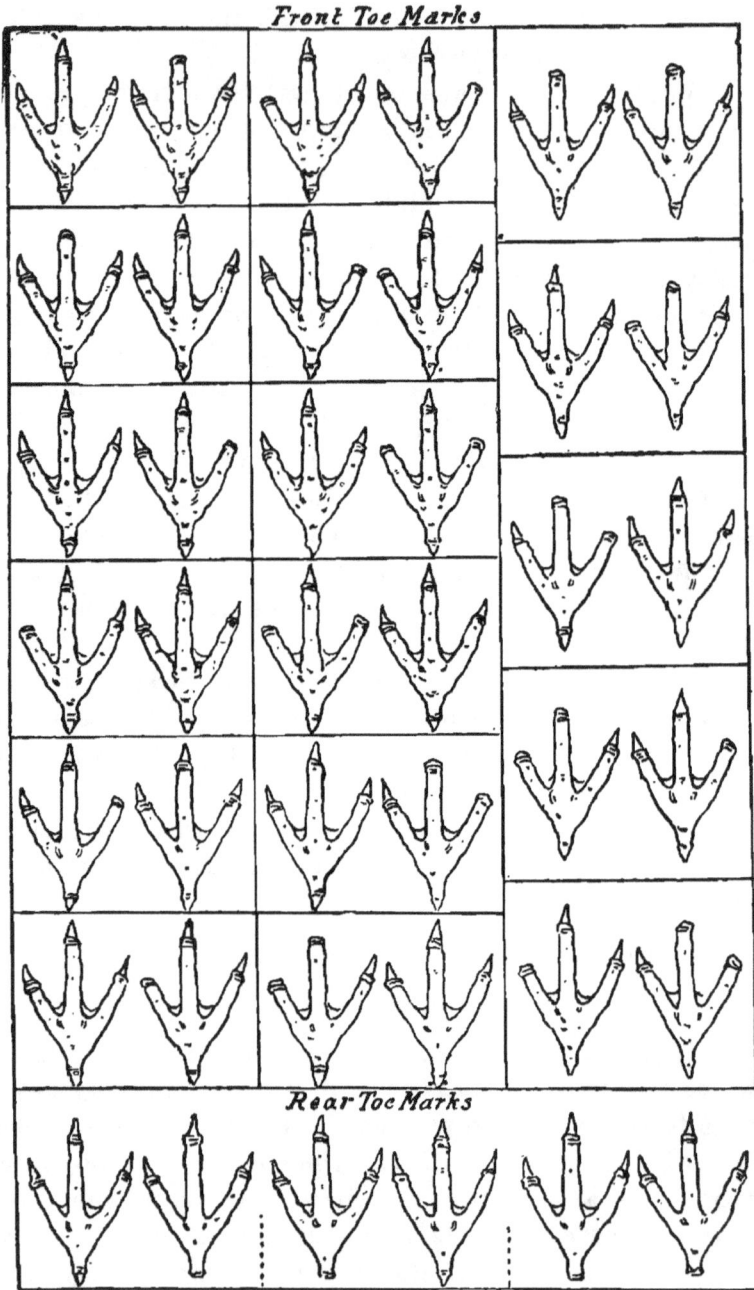

FIG. 24. SUGGESTIONS FOR MARKING TURKEYS BY THEIR FEET.

season. The first night a flock fails to return to its home roost, it should be looked up, separated from the other flocks and driven home. To do this is comparatively easy if immediately attended to, but each day they run together makes their separation more difficult.

To readily distinguish their own birds, many raisers try to have turkeys of a different color from any of those of their neighbors. By breeding for several seasons from a gobbler of a breed different from those kept near by, the flock takes on characteristics of its own, and each individual is readily distinguished. The White, Buff, Slate and Red or Golden varieties are valued principally for such use by growers. An additional advantage is gained, because first crosses between pure breeds are much more hardy, and some combinations are much larger. The grading up of common stock by the repeated use of males of a pure breed also improves its profitable qualities.

This means of identifying a flock is an excellent one, but is not sufficient for all purposes, for it is often desirable to distinguish the birds of a flock from each other, the stock raised one year from that of another, or that of a favorite hen or gobbler. Your turkeys may be lost among similar colored birds, or they may be captured by thieves, and dressed before you get a clue to them. If you have a private mark you can tell them, dead or alive. A private brand is desirable, for many reasons.

In turkey-raising sections, where there is a flock on nearly every farm, a system of marking their feet is followed. This is done by clipping off one or more of their nails, or tips of their toes, as soon as the little turkeys are hatched. At this age they take very little notice of the operation, and there is little or no bleeding. Each raiser has a different mark, and in some towns these are registered at the town clerk's office, the same as the brands of sheep or cattle. As a turkey has three front and one back toes on each foot, or eight toes altogether, many different brands may be made by clipping the different toes. The illustration on Page 88 shows some of them.

Six different marks may be made by clipping only one front toe. Nine more by clipping but two front toes. By clipping either the right or left back toe, the number may be doubled or trebled. By clipping more toes, combinations almost without number may be made, but it will be rarely necessary to remove more than one to two nails, even in a turkey-growing section.

Should mature turkeys thus marked be stolen and dressed, they may be identified, as the marks cannot be changed without showing the fresh mutilation. The marks of little turkeys may be changed without detection, provided sufficient time passes to allow them to heal before they are examined. The more toes you clip, the more difficult it is to change your marks.

Other marks, in addition to the foot marks, are sometimes necessary. The beak may be filed, holes punched in the skin or web of the wing, or a loop of colored silk fastened in the flesh where it can not be seen. Although you may feel that such a precaution is not necessary in your case, probably if you follow this practice, you will at some time be very glad that you have done so.

CHAPTER XII.

HINDRANCES AND DISEASES.

The chief hindrances and obstacles to turkey growing are human and animal thieves, lice and disease. You can always find a market for your dressed turkeys; you can generally make satisfactory arrangements with your neighbors, if your birds trespass upon their land; but all the obstacles may be overcome by patience, perseverance and intelligence. In the more thickly settled portions of the country, thieves are the worst enemies the poultry grower has. In some parts of New England, poultry thieving seems to be a profession with some people, as our court records, when a culprit is caught, will show. But these thieves rarely steal in their own neighborhood. They center in some large town or city, and go out by night, with teams, five, ten, and sometimes twenty miles in their predatory excursions. If your turkeys roost out of doors, it will be necessary to keep one or more dogs to warn you of the approach of the thieves. You cannot shoot them as you can foxes and coyotes, but you can do something which the thieves dread more than the shot gun; cause their arrest. As your action must be determined by the laws of the place where you live, no further advice can be given than always to bear in mind that eternal vigilance is the price of success in turkey raising.

Of animals, dogs do more mischief than foxes. If you cannot cure your dog of worrying turkeys, shoot him. For other animals, the gun, traps and poison, judiciously used, are effective remedies.

Lice, a great annoyance to the poultry keeper, may be **ex**terminated from your flock, if they get possession, but it is easier to keep them away. If the sitting hen or turkey has been treated with insect powder, as advised in the chapter on Incubation, no lice will be on the mother or in the nest to begin work on the newly hatched poult. But if they do come,—and they may in spite of all precautions,—you must quickly rid the birds of them or your losses will be great. If the young turkey begins to droop, refuses to eat, and acts depressed, at once examine the head for lice. You may find three or four large brown ones half buried in the flesh. Remove them and rub the head with sweet oil, or fresh lard mixed with kerosene. Examine, also, the ends of the wings. There you may find some large gray lice, which must be treated in like manner. If you know that all insects, from the largest dragon fly to the minutest hen louse, have no lungs like animals, but breathe through countless pores in their skin,—the same as though we breathed through the pores in our skin instead of through our nostrils,—then you must know that anything which closes those pores quickly, produces suffocation. The best two things known to do that are oil and Pyrethrum (Persian insect powder). Neither produces any harm to lung-breathing creatures. Having applied the oil to the head and the wings, throroughly apply Pyrethrum to the rest of the body by means of a little blower, which can be obtained at a drug store. Also dust the mother turkey at night the same way. Never use sulphur on young turkeys. Carefully watch your flock, and if you detect the lice again, go through the same operation. When the poults are fully feathered and have "thrown the red," they can wander about and keep the lice away themselves. If the broods are cooped, thoroughly scald their coops with boiling suds; burn the litter in them, replacing it with a fresh supply. Filth will soon make short work of them. Feed on clean surfaces. Give them full liberty on dry, warm days, and keep a space of dry sand at all times convenient, for grit and dust.

PREVENTION OF DISEASES.

Although the greatest trouble in raising turkeys may be due to a lack of vigor or hardiness,—the result of breeding from young, inferior or closely related stock,—there is no question but that turkeys, as well as other living creatures, are liable to be destroyed by diseases which even the most vigorous may not escape, if exposed to the most virulent form. Overfeeding, underfeeding, lack of exercise and various influences may make individuals more susceptible, but certain infections are so powerful as to overcome even the strongest and finest specimens.

The Rhode Island Experiment Station says: "Cholera, scarlet fever, diphtheria, and many other serious diseases which affect man, are all prevented from becoming general by nearly the same means. These diseases are propagated by germs given off by the patient. If infected persons are not immediately separated from the well, and isolated,—prevented from coming in contact with others,—they would cause an epidemic, which, once well started, might sweep the country.. Not only are such patients kept in quarantine, but those who care for them are also prevented from coming in direct contact with the well. When the disease has run its course, the patient, the attendants, the rooms occupied, and every article that the germs may have come in contact with, are disinfected,—cleansed with some solution that kills germs. If this is properly done, all of the germs within doors are destroyed. If this were not done, every one using the same rooms, clothing or articles in the room, would be liable to infection, even a long time after the patient had vacated the premises. Germs of disease may dry up, and, if not destroyed, again become active a long time after, if given suitable soil to grow in. They grow faster and multiply with greater rapidity in some soils, and, as in the case of weeds grown in sand and rich loam, the ranker the growth, the more rapidly they spread, the greater the

94 TURKEY CULTURE.

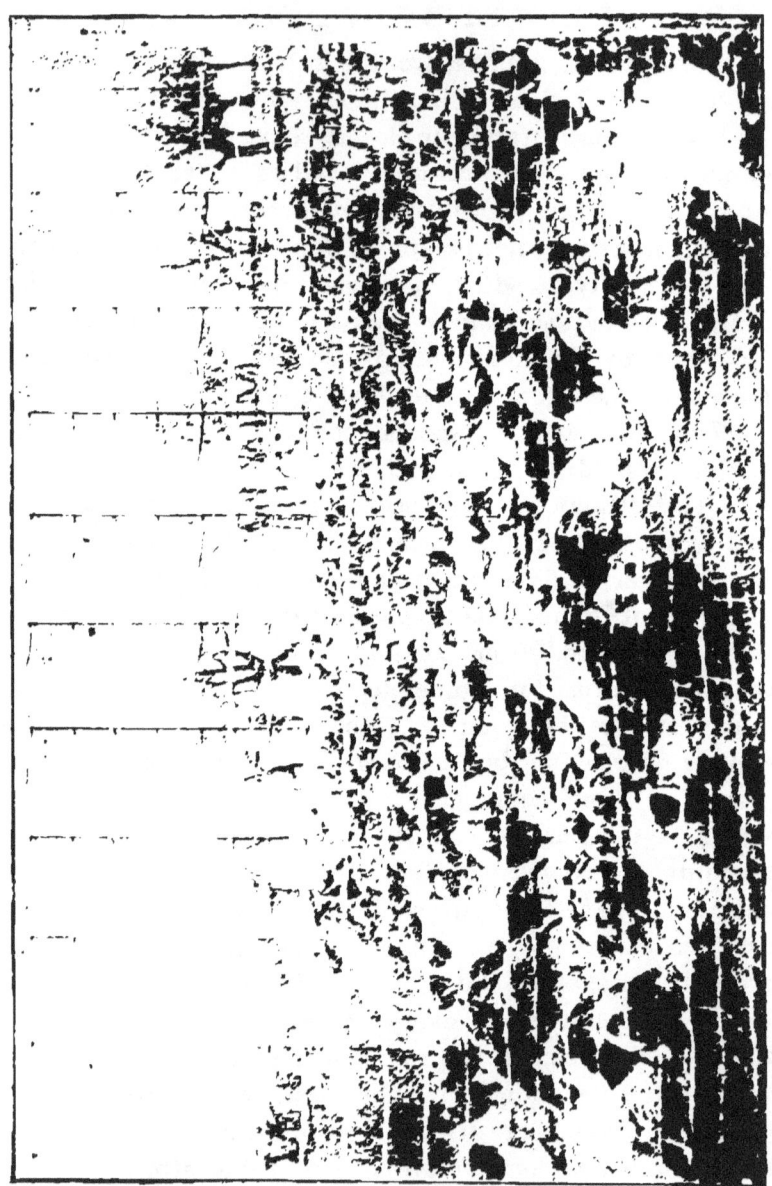

FIG. 25. NO MORE TROUBLE FROM STRAYING TURKEYS.

This illustration shows Mr. Dawley's turkey park, described on Page 112 of this book. The fence illustrated above is a cheap but very durable affair made solely by the Page Woven Wire Fence Co., of Adrian, Mich.

number of germs thrown off and the greater their power. Living surfaces having healthy secretions are poor soils for germs, while abnormal secretions may enable them to thrive. Filth and decaying matter nourish certain germs. Healthy organs resist and may destroy a certain quantity of disease germs, but may be overcome by a much greater number.

"Purchasing birds here and there in making up a flock, may bring all sorts of diseases and parasites together, thus infecting a place at the start to such an extent that it is hard to get rid of them. Each new bird should be thoroughly examined for disease of any kind and treated for lice before being allowed to run with others. A few days' quarantine is very desirable. Do not buy birds showing the slightest trace of disease. Avoid all that are suspicious, for a mild case of disease may introduce a serious trouble. Keep your flocks away from those of your neighbors, as a single infected fowl or turkey may infect a dozen or more different flocks, if allowed to run with them on common ground. Isolate your own stock from that of others as completely as possible. Do not feed uncooked offal. Entrails of animals are liable to contain parasites and germs of disease that will affect fowls, therefore should be long and well cooked before being fed to any living thing. Do not feed milk from cows that are suspected of having tuberculosis. Do not allow persons having consumption to expectorate where they are. Every fowl which dies from any cause should be subjected to post-mortem examination. Persons making such examination should make sure that the skin of their hands is not cut or abraded. This would make them liable to receive infectious matter that might result in blood poisoning. All instruments used in post-mortem examinations should, as well as the hands, be afterwards cleansed in a solution of some antiseptic, like carbolic acid. By such examinations a disease may be discovered before it becomes very prevalent. It is best to sacrifice inferior and sickly specimens, as they are usually the first to become infected, and are apt to become disease breeders. Carcasses of diseased birds should be promptly buried, deep under ground, in a location remote from the haunts of fowls or animals, or, better still, boiled or burned, that the infectious germs may be destroyed. Coops or buildings that have been occupied by them, or the ground where they have lain, should be thoroughly sprayed or drenched with a solution of copperas or carbolic acid. The great benefit in doctoring fowls whose worth is but a few dollars, lies principally in the preventive treatment of large numbers at one time. An early diagnosis of a disease makes this possible. But one has to be on the alert to observe signs of sickness on first appearance, and something of an expert to recognize what it is, the cause and cure.

"Immediate isolation and disinfection should be as promptly enforced in the case of diseased turkeys as with diseased persons. Every infected flock is a menace to other flocks. Kill and burn, or bury deep, all diseased birds, disinfect that which they have contaminated, if possible, and remove the survivors to fresh, uncontaminated land, and keep this up. Other turkeys should be prevented from going onto the infected land. This, in combination with the use of vigorous stock only, bred and fed and cared for according to the best methods, should do away with the mortality among turkeys."

DIARRHŒA.—Of diseases, the most to be dreaded are diarrhœa and roup, when the turkeys are fed and housed like fowls. Diarrhœa attacks the young, and is caused by exposure to cold and wet, lack of grit with their food, sour, uncooked food, access to stagnant water, etc. Give scalded milk to drink, and feed on hard-boiled eggs, stale bread crumbs and boiled rice, according to your convenience. Never give "sloppy" food. Use black pepper freely. Some of our essayists keep on hand and use occasionally whole black pepper, for its wholesome properties. Adult turkeys taken with diarrhœa can be fed with boiled rice, and thus cured. I have cured a whole flock by the use of the Douglas Mixture alone.*

ROUP is one of the most to be dreaded of all diseases which afflict poultry. It rarely affects turkeys that are not housed, pampered, or overfed, or that do not run with fowls. The prominent cause is exposure to cold and wet. So prominent is this, that the disease may be properly called malignant catarrh. It is worse than influenza in human beings. Prevention is better than cure. The confinement necessary to properly doctor roup would spoil r turkey. Kill and bury the first case. Wring the necks or the diseased ones and bury them so deeply that no disease germs from them ever could come to the surface. Never cut off the head of a roupy fowl; the very blood is poison. If any of the pus from a diseased bird gets into your eyes or on your hand where the skin is abraded, trouble will ensue. Dry quarters for the young turkeys; clean, wholesome food and free range when the grass is not wet, will keep your flock free from this scourge, if they are kept away from diseased stock or contaminated premises.

The importance of this subject impels me to subjoin the following extract from the publication of the *Fanciers' Review* called "Five Hundred Questions and Answers on Poultry Raising." It is a well-known fact that exposure to cold and wet will cause—1. Roup, as more correctly stated, will produce acute inflammatory action and resulting exudation, eventually embracing the entire surface of the membranes of the nose, mouth, throat and windpipe. If this exudation is not speedily checked, it degenerates into

---

* Following is the formula for the Douglas Mixture:
  Sulphuric acid, 2 ounces
  Sulphate of iron (copperas), ½ pound
  Water, 2 gallons

Keep in a stone jug or vessel. Add one tablespoonful to every quart of water in the drinking vessel.

pus, which is the discharge present in the last two stages of roup, and is the only mode in which this disease is disseminated.

2. In this stage, termed diphtheritic roup, the exudative membrane, becoming permanent and pressing upon the subjacent tissue, acts as a foreign body, causing ulcerations to appear on the surface. These ulcerations are the so-called "cankers."

3. This condition arrived at, there is a stagnation of the nutritive processes, the blood becomes impaired, and scrofula and liver disease supervene.

These conclusions have been arrived at after studying the disease for three years, during which time diseased fowls have been experimented upon, killing some at the various stages and dissecting them. They are easily cured in the first stage, curable in the second, and not worth curing in the third.

The following will be found to be unequaled treatment for all stages of the disease, combined with **nutritious**, soft food:

Pills.—Sulphate of copper, half grain; cayenne pepper, one grain; hydrastine, half grain; copaiba, three drops; Venetian turpentine, quarter section. In pill, night and morning.

Lotion.—Sulphate of copper quarter ounce, dissolved in a pint of rain water. To wash out the mouth and nostrils, if required.

The simplest means of preventing their drinking water acting as a means of spreading the disease, is to add a little tar water to it, prepared by stirring about one pound of tar in two gallons of water and decanting the clear water as required for use.

GAPES.—These are very fine red worms found in the trachea or windpipe of young birds, most destructive to chicks when they are from three to six weeks old. On many farms in Rhode Island, gapes had caused the death of fifty

HINDRANCES AND DISEASES.

per cent of little turkeys for years, and many who suffered such losses, while they realized the cause, were ignorant that much could be done to prevent or cure the trouble. It attacks all other poultry, also, being most prevalent in July and August. The chief symptoms are a suppressed cough and a peculiar gasping, from which the malady is named. As many as twenty or thirty of these worms, averaging five-eighths of an inch in length, have been found attached to the mucous membrane of the trachea, which, together with the lungs, was badly inflamed. This so-called forked worm in reality consists of a male and female permanently united. Their food is the blood of their host, which also gives them a red appearance. The matured female contains several thousand eggs, which emerge only after her death. It has been said that the eel-like embryos never leave the eggs while they are within the living body of the mother, however complete the development of both may be, and that only by the death of the female and the destruction of its body are the ova placed at liberty. Late investigations dispute this statement. The embryo will emerge from the egg if the surrounding medium offers favorable conditions. These are moisture and a temperature of at least 68 degrees Fahrenheit. In a moist state, the eggs pre-

FIG. 26. THE GAPEWORM. Four times natural size. The large worm is the male, the smaller one the female.

serve their vitality for months, or even a year, if the temperature is kept below 59 degrees Fahrenheit, but under these conditions the contents of the eggs eventually become dissolved. If placed in a dry medium, like dry sand, their contents dry up the more rapidly in proportion to the elevation of the temperature. If an unimpaired egg is kept moist and subjected to a temperature of 77 degrees, the embryo within the egg moves and turns about and finally escapes by pushing away one of the coverlets. Twenty-eight to thirty days of such a degree of warmth, with moisture, is sufficient for the development of the embryo and its escape from the shell. These embryos live in water, where they swim about in a serpentine manner. They have been kept alive at this stage almost a year by subjecting them to a low temperature, but with a temperature of from 68 to 77 degrees, they did not live more than eight or ten days. The illustrations, Figs. 26 and 27, reproduced from report of United States Bureau of Animal Industry, 1884, represent the various stages from the egg to the mature worm attached to the trachea.

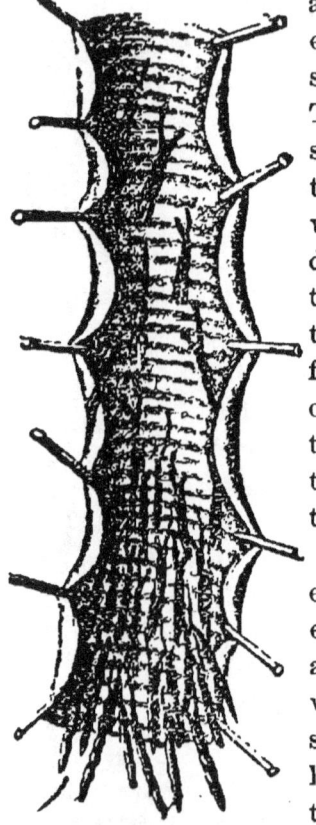

FIG. 27. WINDPIPE OF A FOWL.
Slit open and pinned back to show a large number of the gapeworms attached to the inside, natural size.

Fowls become infected in several ways, food and water containing eggs or the live embryos being probably the two most common. The vitality of gapeworm eggs is very strong and may be preserved for a long time in the soil or wherever the eggs may fall. Birds affected with this malady frequently expel, in a fit of coughing, plump gapeworms full of eggs. Other fowls near by consume with avidity the worms thus ejected. Two or three weeks later these same young fowls are sure to present symptoms of the malady. Dr. H. D. Walker has pointed out that earthworms act the part of host to the gapeworm embryo, and believes that they are the prime means of spreading the gapes. More recent experiments show that while earthworms in infected soils often contain the embryos, the earthworm is not a necessary host, because the disease is found where earthworms are not natural to the soil. Dr. Walker still maintains that if chicks are kept from eating earthworms, they will not have the gapes. He argues that without the aid of earthworms to carry gapeworms below the first line, they would soon be exterminated in the North. He admits that chicks fed on fresh eggs of the gapeworm might not contract the disease, but thinks it is perhaps because their digestion is so rapid that the eggs pass off before they have time to hatch. Older chicks are not so susceptible, because they have more power to dislodge the worms from the trachea, and are not embarrassed by a few.

Wherever gape-infected chicks or poults have long been kept, the ground becomes infected with the germs, and remains infected just as long as chickens are kept there. Curing the birds will not remove the infection, but if no poultry are kept for a sufficient length of time, the infection dies out for want of necessary conditions for development. It is folly to put young chicks on a plat of ground or field infected with gapeworms, unless the soil is freed from contamination. This can be done by spreading half a bushel of fresh air-slaked lime on every hundred square feet of ground. Chicks kept in pens for eight weeks, the soil of which has thus been purified, usually escape infection. The same quantity of coarse salt may be used in place of the lime, but it must be dissolved by water or rain before the chicks are put in, or they may eat it and die. Avoid giving water from an infected source. For destroying the infection in the soil, water containing a large quantity of salicylic acid or sulphuric acid is recommended by Megnin.

There are many very old and effective remedies for removing gapeworms. Air-slaked lime has long been used and has been found to promptly remove the worms from the trachea. Afflicted chickens are placed in a box, which is covered with a sheet of thin muslin. On this muslin is placed a handful of air-slaked lime, the muslin is then jarred to cause the dust of the lime to fall through, which enters the lungs of the chickens and causes them to cough off the worms. The lime is supposed to affect the worms, which release their hold or do not retain so strong a hold on the windpipe. This is said to do no harm to the chick and to be a sure cure.

Another old-fashioned method of treatment, which seems to have been quite generally followed with great success, is to confine the chickens to a canvas-covered box while they are fumigated with the fumes of carbolic acid. The fumes are produced by pouring a teaspoonful of carbolic acid on a red-hot brick placed in the corner of the box. If there is glass in one end of the box, the chickens will huddle against it and keep away from the corner where the brick is, while their actions may be watched through the glass. If the fumes seem too dense, ventilation may be given. A minute is usually long enough to expose them to the fumes. By the use of a sliding door in the box, the chickens may be driven into the box from their coop in any number desired. An upper compartment for the chickens, having a slat floor, under which the acid is burned, would be most satisfactory where a large number are to be handled. Dr. Roth, Mrs.

FIG. 28. CÆCA Of healthy turkey, the central tube being the small intestine, while the two wings comprise the blind gut or cæca.

Carson, and many others, have long followed this plan of treatment with great success. The only objection to it is that if the chickens are fumigated too long, they may be killed, as well as the worms. This treatment is also valuable for the cure of roup. Another common practice is to drop six drops of strong salt and water down the windpipe with a feather, as it will quickly and surely cure them, and is simple and not as severe as most other remedies. Camphor and water, camphorated sweet oil and crude petroleum, are each recommended; one drop in the windpipe from a medicine dropper, oil can or feather, is said to be all that is necessary to kill and cause the removal of the worms. A feather stripped of its web, except at the tip, and moistened with a mixture of sweet oil and turpentine, is used by some. It is inserted in the windpipe, and twisted as it is withdrawn.

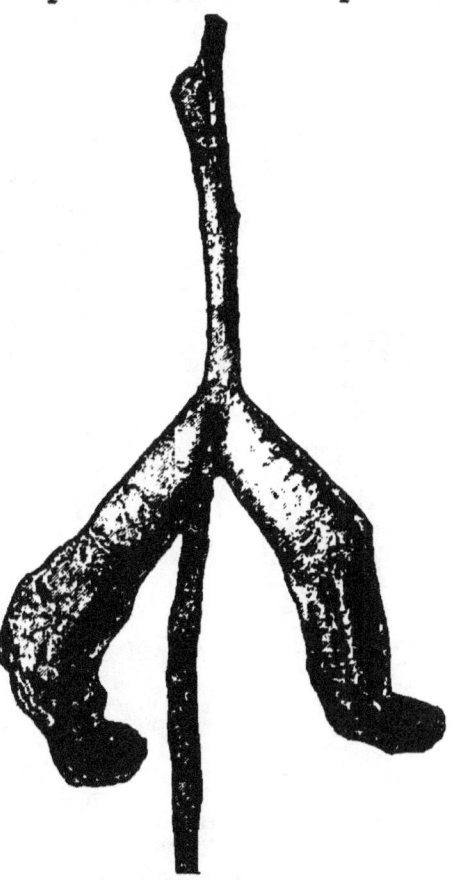

FIG. 29. DISEASED CÆCA
Of turkey, thickened, enlarged and ulcerated in "blackhead" disease.

Worms may be destroyed in this way, but it is not practicable where large numbers of chickens are to be treated. Some poultry keepers simply apply turpentine externally to the mouths or throats of the chickens having gapes. Fine tobacco, petroleum or kerosene, turpentine assafœtida and alum, all have been recommended for mixing with the feed, to prevent and stamp out the gape disease. M. Megnin gives each pheasant seven and one-half grains of assafœtida combined with the same quantity of pulverized yellow gentian in their feed. Five to ten drops of turpentine to a pint of meal and made into dough, is used by some. When garlic or onions are faithfully fed, the trouble is much reduced. The explanation is that the volatile part of these substances, being absorbed into the system, is thrown off through the lungs and brought into contact with the parasitic worms in the windpipe, to which it is fatal, and they are ejected with the mucous. Megnin recommends adding about fifteen grains of salicylic acid to each quart of the drinking water. Prevention is better than a cure. The importance of the total destruction of the parasites after their removal, should be realized. If the worms are killed and thrown upon the ground, it is scarcely likely that the mature eggs will have sustained any injury. Decomposition will set free the eggs, the young embryos escape and enter the soil, and ultimately may find their way into the air passages of some bird. The worms, as well as the dead bodies of anything affected with them, should be burned, if we wish to prevent the spread of the disease. If infected birds are buried, earthworms or skunks may bring the infection to the surface.

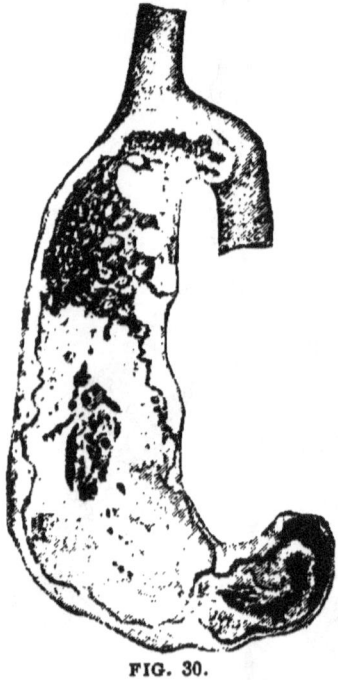

FIG. 30.
One side or wing of the cæcum cut open, showing its diseased state.

Pools and wet places are supposed to be favorable to the preservation and development of these germs. It has often

HINDRANCES AND DISEASES.

been observed that gapes are more prevalent during a wet spring and during those summers following a mild winter. In stamping out this trouble, the importance of the addition of a small quantity of some germicide like carbolic acid, salicylic acid, assafœtida or petroleum to the drinking water, sufficient to destroy worms or eggs that are ejected therein, should not be overlooked.

"BLACKHEAD" IN TURKEYS IS CONTAGIOUS.

For more than fifteen years there has been great loss among turkeys raised in southern New England, from a supposed contagious disease known as "blackhead." It has entirely prevented turkey raising on many farms, and has caused great destruction. Public attention was first directed to this disease by Prof. Cushman of the Rhode Island Experiment Station, in the summer of 1893. The matter was closely followed

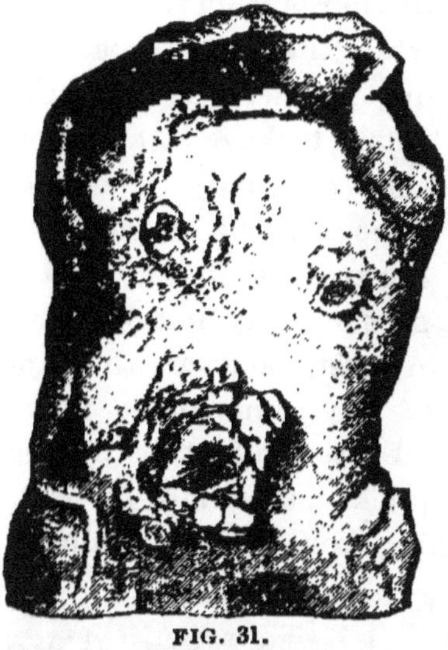

FIG. 31.
One cæcum from Fig. 29, slit open to show thickened mucous membrane.

FIG. 32.
The other cæcum from Fig. 29, cut crosswise to show thickening.

at that institution until the work was taken by the United States Bureau of Animal Industry. A report on it appeared in Bulletin 8 from that Bureau, which illustrated and described the disease, and indicated that it might be infectious. Circular No. 5, just issued by V. A. Moore, Chief of the Bureau of Animal Pathology, gives later results, showing conclusively that blackhead is contagious. Not only is this true, but instead of being confined to the New England coast, certain flocks in the Middle and

Western States are affected. The disease has extended into the Western States, though not yet found in the South, while the losses of Eastern turkey growers from this source alone are very large. Evidence accumulates that the entire Northern third of the country is sprinkled with infected districts. The disease is usually accompanied by a diarrhœal discharge from the bowels, while the head turns dark or purple. It attacks young turkeys at all ages, and gradually develops. More turkeys succumb to the trouble in the latter part of July and early in August, and at the approach of cold weather, than at any other time. The affected birds seem able to hold out against it during warm, dry weather, but they quickly succumb in wet, stormy weather. The turkeys dying from blackhead almost invariably have a disease of the liver and a part of the intestine. The turkey is infected early in life, and infection does not take place later on; hence, it may be transmitted from old to young. The disease apparently first affects the cæcum or pronged part of the lower bowel, which becomes thickened and enlarged and badly ulcerated. The liver is also spotted, and in advanced stages is covered with circular areas, showing destruction of tissue within the organ (see Figs. 28 to 34 inclusive). The

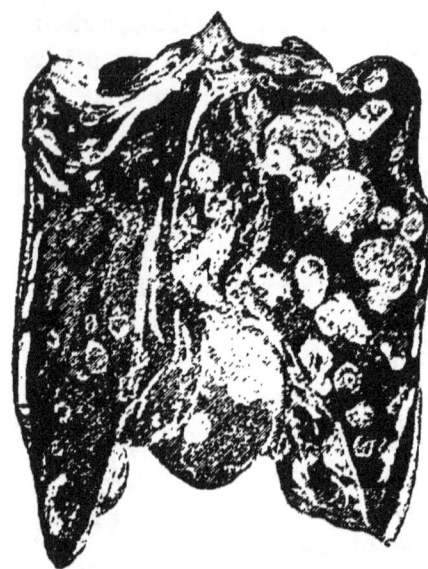

FIG. 33.
Spotted liver due to "blackhead."

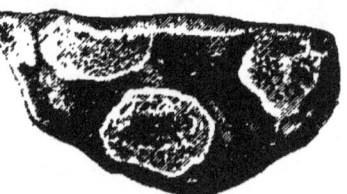

FIG. 34.
Natural size of spots on liver.

changes in the liver and bowel are so pronounced when it causes death that turkey raisers may in many instances learn whether their own turkeys are affected by examining those that die. Blackhead is a hitherto undetermined disease, and is caused by a minute organism, which places the malady among the infectious diseases. It is now demonstrated that turkeys contract the disease from the droppings of diseased birds. Hence sick birds must not remain with the breeding birds, nor should stock be obtained from infected sections. Broods of young turkeys should be kept away from buildings where turkeys have passed the winter, and be kept on ground uncontaminated by the droppings of diseased turkeys or suspicious breeding stock. The droppings from all roosting places should be frequently and thoroughly collected, and the place well dusted with air-slaked lime. If the disease is known to exist in the flock, sprinkle the premises liberally with a mixture of crude carbolic acid one-half gallon and crude sulphuric acid one-half gallon, to which twenty gallons of water are added. The droppings collected may be dusted thoroughly with air-slaked lime, and mixed with several times their bulk of muck or loam, to absorb the ammonia that would otherwise escape, and thus become a valuable fertilizer. Turkeys should not be fed on the same spot of ground day after day, but as far as possible in a new place every day, that the danger of infection through the food and droppings may be lessened. Dr. Moore's circular suggests that those who have recently had this disease in their flocks should dispose of their old turkeys and begin new by hatching turkey eggs under hens, or with turkeys obtained from non-infected districts, "preferably from the South, as this disease is not known to exist there."

PREVALENCE OF TAPEWORMS IN TURKEYS.

PROF. SAMUEL CUSHMAN.

Our work with the disease known as "blackhead" enabled us to examine the intestines of each bird the entire length for tapeworms, and we found that they were more generally infested than we had even suspected. Turkeys affected with blackhead were free from tapeworms, but of the sixty-five examined that showed no traces of that disease, the intestines of forty contained tapeworms. Worms from a quarter of an inch to several inches in length were found, and occasionally those a foot or more long. Some birds contained only great numbers of very minute worms in the upper intestine, others only large fully developed worms in the lower intestine, while in still others small ones were found in the upper, and numbers of long and large ones in the lower intestine. In one or two instances these worms were found only in the blind prolongation of the lower intestine. One bird found in a dying condition in a flock from which turkeys had been dying for over a month, and from which thirty had been lost within a week, was found to contain a very large number of tapeworms of medium size, and no other cause for sickness could be discovered. Frequently the lower part of the intestine was fairly crowded with great numbers of long worms. One little turkey three or four weeks old had many small worms in the duodenum, and the remainder of the intestines was almost completely filled with those that were several inches long, about fifty in number. A microscopical examination of apparently mature segments by Dr. Smith, showed that ripe embryos were present. As these sick turkeys come from many different farms in various parts of the State, and but one or two birds were secured from any one place, it seems that this trouble is very prevalent among young turkeys during the summer months in Rhode Island, and this may account for loss of turkeys that is often reported from other sections.

I am convinced that tapeworms cause the death of great numbers of little turkeys, and that some suitable worm medicine should be frequently given them throughout the season. Turkeys are troubled with tapeworms from early spring until late in the fall, and sometimes have spasms from this cause. Very young turkeys suffer the most. After they are three months old they are better able to withstand the injurious effect. The worms apparently irritate the bowels, causing digestive derangement, diarrhœa, weakness and death. At certain seasons, segments of worms may be found early in the morning under the roosts among the droppings of the infected turkeys. Evidently the younger they receive the parasites, the more they suffer. Doubtless if the birds survive until the embryos have developed and have mostly passed out, they may gradually recover. A few worms may do little harm, while a great number may be fatal.

How the young receive the embryos in the spring is an interesting question. Whether snails, worms or insects harbor them and thus scatter the infection, or whether they receive the infection from the droppings of old turkeys, is yet to be determined. Dr. Stiles, of the United States Bureau of Animal Industry, says that ten different species of tapeworms from chickens are described by investigators, and that according to certain Italian authors two species—one of them the most common of all—pass their larval stage in the house fly.

Another species, it is said, has for its intermediate hosts various slugs, while another has a snail as its host. Dr. Salmon thinks it will be found that earthworms, insects and snails are the intermediate hosts for these tapeworm embryos, and that there is, at present, no reason for thinking they will be able to develop without some intermediate host.

In whatever way young turkeys receive the embryos of these parasites, doubtless they may be promptly freed from them, and any injurious results prevented, by the frequent use of simple worm medicines in their food or water. The longer infected turkeys have been kept on a farm, and the greater the number annually grown, the more thoroughly will tapeworm eggs be sown upon the land, and if slugs, snails and earthworms are their intermediate host, the more generally will the turkeys contain infecting embryos. Where there have been no tapeworm eggs, snails and earthworms will not harbor the embryos, and young turkeys will not become infected in this way. If we can keep turkeys free from worms we will prevent them from sowing the seed for the tapeworm crop; therefore, dosing the breeding turkeys in the winter and spring would be a preventive measure. Raise the little turkeys on fresh, uncontaminated land that chickens or other turkeys have not run upon for years, and give them an occasional dose that will destroy tapeworm and gapeworm embryos. Give up keeping turkeys, either old or young, on ground infested for several years. Confine infected flocks to an inclosure, and treat them with worm medicine until they are free from worms; meanwhile, frequently disinfect the ground in the pen, to destroy the eggs that pass off. Then move them to new ground. If it is found that wild birds, or any of the animals that wander over the same ground, harbor the same tapeworms, additional measures will have to be taken to entirely stamp out the infection.

Which of the well-known remedies for tapeworms in animals is best suited to the turkey, and what amount should be given to turkeys at different ages, are questions that naturally arise. Until we can advise on this matter from knowledge gained by practical experience, we leave it for turkey raisers to test for themselves. Probably the best results may be expected from the use of freshly powdered kousso or cusso. According to the

United States Dispensatory, the treatment for a human being is, for an adult half an ounce; for a child of six years, one-fourth ounce; taken in the morning upon an empty stomach. A previous evacuation of the bowels is recommended, and should the medicine not act on the bowels in three or four hours, a brisk cathartic should be administered. One dose is usually sufficient to destroy the worms. Should the quantity mentioned not prove effective, the dose may be doubled. Kousso seems to act only

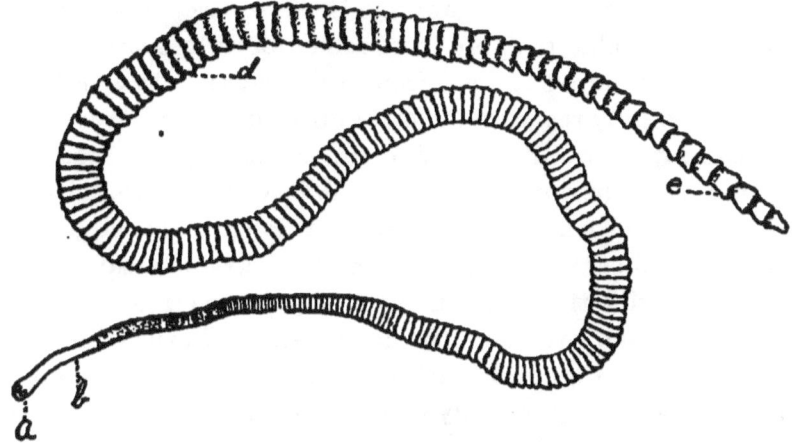

FIG. 35. TAPEWORM FROM A TURKEY.

Illustration of one selected from about fifty found in a turkey three or four weeks old. There is so little known about tapeworms of fowls, and so much confusion as to description and classification, that experts have been unable to identify it. *a*, head; *b*, neck; *c, d* and *e*, segments in various stages of development. The segments or joints are formed next to the head, are gradually pushed back by the growth of new segments, and finally become terminal (*e*), where they mature, separate and pass away. Each adult segment contains complete male and female organs, and when it separates from the main body, is full of embryos, which are supposed to find their way into some temporary host before they reach their final host, the turkey.—*Rhode Island Experiment Station.*

as a poison to the worms, and is said not to seriously affect the patient. Koussein or kosin, the active principle of kousso, is highly recommended, two scruples being the dose for a man.

Male fern is an effective remedy, but an overdose is a distinct poison. Six drams of the oil have caused the death of a person. It has been known to cause blindness in the lower animals, and should be used with extreme caution. It is often given in combination with castor oil. Tansy is much used as a preventive, and powdered areca nut is used for the removal of tapeworms from dogs and other animals. The latter is frequently combined with male fern. Ground pumpkin seed is also used as a remedy.

The dose of these remedies would have to be much reduced for turkeys. Turkey raisers may administer very light doses to a few turkeys, and larger doses to others, and thus learn how great a quantity may be given to healthy turkeys with impunity. It is to be hoped that many may be able to apply these remedies with success, and immediately prevent loss from this cause. Assafœtida, which is highly recommended for preventing and overcoming the gapeworm disease of fowls, is also said to possess virtues as a tapeworm remedy. This is administered either in the food or water. M. Megnin, a French investigator, gave each pheasant seven and one-half grains assafœtida, combined with the same quantity of pulverized gentian, in their food, and overcame the gapeworms. Turpentine administered in slight quantities in the food is recommended by some, and may possibly enable the turkey raiser to kill both parasites.

LIVER DISEASE.—Turkeys may have enlargement and other non-contagious diseases of the liver if inbred, overfed, given too little chance for exercise, etc. All suspected birds should be immediately slaughtered, examined and buried.

LEG WEAKNESS.—Caused either by inherited constitutional weakness, wrong food or bad management. Clean such specimens out of your flock at once and avoid the cause.

HOW TO KEEP TURKEYS AT HOME.

Our illustration on Page 94 shows what is probably the largest turkey ranch in the world. It is owned by F. E. Dawley of Onondaga county, N. Y., who is manager of the farmers' institute work in that State. He raises tur-

HINDRANCES AND DISEASES.   113

keys in a wholesale way, and entirely avoids any trouble from their wandering away by keeping them in a large pasture and orchard, fenced with the Page twenty-five-bar deer park fence, eighty inches high. Many of the young poults are hatched at home in incubators and raised in brooders, and others are hatched on outside farms and brought home in the fall. Their feed is made as nearly as possible to conform to the diet of turkeys roaming at large, by giving butchers' scraps that have been run through a bone mill, to take the place of insects, plenty of succulent green stuff, and a good supply of broken limestone grit. By careful account, Mr. Dawley finds that turkeys which are kept in partial confinement will lay on flesh at a less cost per pound than those which roam without restraint, and the quality is much better. One of the most profitable lessons learned from Mr. Dawley's experience is, that those who have had to give up turkey raising because of the damage their birds have done to berries, grain or other growing crops, can again take it up, and by building a park with this Page deer park fence, keep their flocks enclosed during the season that they would do damage, and let them out after the crops are harvested. They will not fly out from a ten-acre enclosure unless by mistake. The eighty-eight-inch fence keeps them, except that one or two may occasionally rise near the center of the field and soar so far that they come down on the outside. This fence is very durable and remarkably cheap. Its merits for fencing in turkey pastures should be known by all raisers of this profitable fowl. The Page Woven Wire Fence Co., of Adrian, Mich., also make wire fencing of every sort and description for every possible purpose, and will be happy to give particulars, free of cost, to all who will write to them at Adrian, Mich., U. S. A.

One of the most valued parts of this turkey ranch is a series of small yards made with the Page wire fence, in which the laying hen turkeys are kept during the breed-

8

ing season, and let out each day after they have laid. Such a yard as this will pay on nearly every farm where turkeys are kept, because every egg can be secured, there are no losses from crows, skunks, rats or other vermin, and beside this, no time is lost in "hunting turkeys' nests," or "watchin' a blamed hen turkey to her eggs."

This matter of keeping turkeys within bounds is often a most serious one. Of course, turkeys can be marked on their feet, according to the system described on Page 87. Then, too, the system of "shingling," as described on Page 67, can be employed. But the latter is practical only on a small scale for breeding turkeys, while the former involves a lot of work and does not prevent turkeys from straying. Much "bad blood" is often caused between neighbors by the depredations of straying turkeys, and turkeys often stray away and are lost. All these troubles are obviated by the Page deer park fence, and the experience of Mr. Dawley and others indicates that this fencing can be profitably used for such a purpose, while it is also profitable for fencing against other stock.

CHAPTER XIII.

PRIZE ESSAYS ON TURKEY CULTURE.

Selected from one hundred and eighty-seven statements of their practical experience, sent to the *Farm and Home* by men and women in all parts of the country who have achieved large success in raising turkeys for profit.

FIRST-PRIZE ESSAY, BY MRS. A. J. SEXSON, FURNAS COUNTY, NEBRASKA.

The first requisite to successful turkey growing is carefully selected stock for parent birds. Selections of the best, for years, have produced the most improved and profitable breeds of stock. The future stock depends very much upon the parent birds, or their ancestry. Repeated breeding from inferior birds makes inferiority hereditary. After having faithfully tried the White, the Wild Black and the Mammoth Bronze turkeys, I prefer the latter for several reasons. They have proven hardier than the White, are equally strong, more gentle and more easily handled than the Black, less apt to roam far away and with proper care are ready for market at an earlier age than either of the other varieties, and I believe are less liable to disease. After complying with the first condition and having secured large, strong, parent turkeys, at least one year old, see that they are in the right condition for breeding.

Breeding fowls should not be overfat, as the offspring of such fowls are less vigorous. If the hens are young (late hatched) they require more food at breeding time, as they are still growing and immature. If hens are old they should have millet and clover, where it can be grown, and less carbonaceous food in the latter part of the season. Too much corn will produce overfat turkeys, unless they have abundant exercise in insect hunting and plenty of green food. When the laying season begins, usually in March, a watchful lookout for the eggs must be kept. It is natural for all turkeys to hide the nest, but petting will do much toward keeping them near the house. Each egg should be gathered as soon as laid and placed, small end down, on cotton or some soft material and kept in a dry, cool, dark place. If not used at once, they should be turned occasionally, to prevent settling or adhering to the shell. As the eggs are removed daily from the nest, it is better to return a hen's egg, until there are five or six in the nest, as a turkey is suspicious and easily discomfited. My turkeys lay entirely in the grove near the house and arrange their nests with skill themselves, my only task being to protect them from natural wild enemies. The nest should always be dry and large, and on the ground if possible. Fifteen eggs are sufficient for a large hen, and if small, thirteen will give better results. Four weeks, and often thirty days, are required to hatch the eggs. This makes a long period of rest for active Mrs. Turkey, yet she must be compelled to do her work faithfully, consequently should have easy access to an abundance of food and pure water, that she may not be forced to remain too long a time off the nest to procure food, thus allowing the eggs to chill.

CARE OF THE YOUNG.—About the twenty-seventh day I throw a hard-boiled egg, mashed very fine, close to the nest, not into, lest it adhere to an egg, rendering the egg air-tight exactly over the beak of the young turkey, which would prevent his escape from the shell. The mother turkey may eat this egg and the one given the following day or two, if it is not needed for her young, but in case she is hatching, she will use it for the little ones, and this food will often save the first-hatched birds. I have had the mother turkey refuse to leave the nest for three days after the first eggs hatched. If she leaves too soon, the remaining eggs may be placed under hens, or hatched by wrapping in wool and keeping warm near the fire. Should an egg become broken in the nest, the soiled eggs should be carefully washed immediately in warm, but not hot, water, and dried and returned at once to the nest. The trying time in the life of turkeys is the first week, when they require constant watching, then great care until they are eight weeks old, or until the quill feathers are well started. The producing of these feathers seems to weaken the fowl, and exhausts the system, and therefore they need especial treatment to counteract this difficulty.

For the first week, the mother and young must have a warm place, free from draughts of air, free from dampness, and where they will be undisturbed by other fowls.

The first three weeks the food should consist of sweet milk (fresh from the cow is best), very hard-boiled eggs and fine wheat, bread crumbs for the little ones, wheat, corn and fresh water for the mother. Feed the mother first and she will not take much of the egg and bread, which is more expensive. During this time, if the weather be warm and sunshiny, let the mother out during the middle of the day, keeping her near the coop, taking care to shut her in before sunset, as the dew is harmful to the young turks. During the first week the little ones are apt to get onto their backs, from which position they cannot rise, and will die if allowed to thus lie for any length of time. Care must be taken not to place the pens near the hills of the small red or black ants, as these are enemies to young turkeys. They not only attack the head and kill the turkey, but if eaten, will almost instantly choke them to death.

The fourth week the food may consist of oatmeal, sour milk curd in small quantities, cracked wheat and scraps from the table, taking care that the scraps contain nothing salt. Salt, salt meat, brine or salt fish will kill them. After the eighth week, give mother and brood their freedom. Feed only in the morning, and this is not needful if they have access to grain fields.

If a turkey becomes sick, it should be isolated at once from the others, to prevent spread of the disease. Land over which diseased fowls wander will be contaminated and infect other flocks. Turkeys require plenty of pure water and must not be allowed to drink from stagnant pools, as this may produce bowel troubles. It is useless to doctor a very sick turkey—better to kill and bury deep at once. Prevention is better than cure, and if the following dose is given fortnightly, or even monthly, throughout the year, to either turkeys or chickens, there will be little necessity for cholera cure: Two ounces cayenne pepper, two ounces sulphur, two ounces alum and two ounces copperas. Mix all together and add two tablespoonfuls to eight quarts of corn meal, and wet the mixture with sweet milk or warm water. This will feed forty fowls.

One may profitably practice giving two broods of young turkeys to one mother when hatched at the same time, as one turkey can hover from twenty-five to thirty little ones during the critical period in their lives, after which they do not need much hovering. The other mother, after being closely confined out of sight and hearing of the little ones for one week, will quickly mate and lay again. This is very practicable and desirable when the first broods are hatched in May, or earlier, as the second hatchings are often the best, only a little later ready for market.

SECOND PRIZE ESSAY.

BY MRS. C. P. SUTTON, TRUMBULL COUNTY, OHIO.

How will I make a start! Buy a trio of turkeys, a tom and two hens, or purchase eggs and set them under hens. My experience favors the former, and three turkey hens will give better results with but little more outlay and care. The extra expense of turkeys over eggs will be amply repaid before the laying season is over. Purchase the stock from a reliable dealer. The tom and hens should not be related or inbred, and should be thick-limbed and compact in size. Select young hens, as they are prolific layers and not so prone to wander. Each fancier has his favorite breed; mine is the Bronze, as they are so quiet and take on flesh rapidly and attain a large size. We sold in January toms hatched in June, which weighed eighteen pounds dressed.

Be careful, in buying turkeys or eggs, not to buy from yards where there has been cholera or other contagious disease. It is much better to buy breeding stock in the fall or early winter, as the stock to select from is larger and prices are lower. The diet, which is of much importance, can also be more carefully attended to as the breeding season approaches. Corn, oats, wheat and buckwheat, with an occasional warm mash until Feb. 1, is good feed. After that date but little corn should be fed, but plenty of oats, bone meal, wheat and milk, as they are muscle- and bone-forming foods. Provide access to pure, clean water at all times, as well as to the dust bath, gravel, oyster shells and lime. Lime insures hard-shelled eggs, which is of great importance. An occasional feed of chopped clover or cabbage leaves is much relished until grass comes. At least once a week give Sheridan's condition powder in their warm feed, one tablespoonful to six turkeys. Also give a teaspoonful of the Douglas mixture in a gallon of drinking water twice a week. My turkeys have access to a shed, and to roosts out of doors, but unless the night is very cold or stormy they do not go into the shed. When new turkeys are taken from the crates, look them over thoroughly for lice, especially in the large hollows between the quill feathers on top of the wings. Dust them plentifully with insect powder.

To insure fertile eggs, mating must occur ten days before laying. A peculiar call, well known to the turkey raiser, announces that the hen is hunting a nest, and now comes the tug of war, for nine out of ten will persist in laying just where they should not, either in the woods, a mile away, or along a stream or swamp. When the turkeys have mated, fix a number of nests by carrying an armful of leaves to clumps of bushes, selecting the site with a view to setting the hen. Never select where they will be in danger of foxes, muskrats or other animals, and when Mrs. Hen starts to seek a nest to deposit her first egg, keep watch of her, and make her lay at least near where you wish her to. If she has stolen a march on you and got a nestful of eggs, shut her up at night and do not liberate her until the next afternoon. When she wants to lay she will probably go straight to her nest. When following her, do so without being seen, for a hen turkey takes the lead for being sly and watchful. If she outwits you, in four weeks from the time you saw her last, if you have young turks, take one in your hand and go near to where you saw her last, and the chirp of the turk you have will bring an answering call from the hen.

You can keep turkeys in any field that has a fence they cannot crawl through, by taking a piece of shingle two inches wide and over each wing hollow out grooves. Take a piece of strong cotton cloth an inch wide, and pass around the wing through the large feathers in the joint next the body and around the grooves, and tie securely, but not too tight, thus fastening the piece of shingle across the back and wings. We never use this except when the hen is turned out with her young turks. Turkey eggs should be kept in a dry, cool place, and turned every day. As soon as the first hen wants to sit, set her and a common hen at the same time, the turkey on eighteen or twenty eggs and the hen on from nine to eleven. Then if they hatch over eighteen, as they should do, place their coops near together and they will run together all the season. If they hatch less, give them all to the turkey. Turkey eggs hatch best on the ground, or low down on a nest prepared by putting in plenty of moist earth. Do not make the nest deep and hollowing, or set the largest hens until they lay the second time, as they are more apt to break the eggs.

Dampen the eggs under common hens frequently with tepid water. You will get little chance at those under the turkey, as they are very close sitters and the less they are interfered with the better. If you wish to move the turkey from where she has laid, take a large slat coop or dish crate, turn it upside down, make a nest at one end, and move the hen at evening, and by morning she will be reconciled to her new quarters. After the first week let her off every two or three days, or she can be left on the four weeks by keeping fresh food and water and the dust bath accessible.

In the wild state, the tom kills all the young turks she can find, hence the desire of the hen for seclusion. It is best for the same person to attend the turkeys during the breeding season, doing everything up as quietly as possible. In about twenty-eight days the little turks will begin to hatch. Do not disturb them the first day. The first feed should be hard boiled egg crumbled fine, or stale bread or crackers, slightly moistened with water, and squeezed dry as possible. After the first two weeks, add rolled oats, oatmeal and cracked wheat, all dry, and clabbered milk scalded and drained in a colander. Add chopped onion or, better, green tops, to the bread or clabbered milk twice a week. Twice a week give a tablespoonful of the condition powders to two quarts of feed. Never feed but little of anything at a time and mix up fresh each time, as turkeys, when young, are small, delicate eaters. We never feed corn meal unless baked and treated like the stale bread. When the turks get their first feed they are removed to a large coop or pen of rails, away from other poultry, and not close to the house or barns. The toe used for a mark should be clipped and treated with the carbolized grease; the top of the head is also greased, and under and top of the wings is dusted with insect powder.

The hen also should be again treated thoroughly for lice, the turkey's greatest enemy. If the turkeys are dying, look for lice. You can scarcely see the large gray ones that burrow deep in the top of the head, and you may look a six-weeks-old turkey all over and not find a louse, when, if you will examine the deep creases on top of the wing, you will find it swarming with big, gray pests. The little turks need clean water, bone meal, gravel and the dust bath. If you have no chopper, buy weekly some stale beef, cut it up, and see how greedily the little turks devour it. Give a few drops of Douglas mixture twice a week in the drinking water or in sweet milk. If the turks show signs of diarrhœa, give a few drops of spiced syrup of rhubarb and powdered chalk with their soft food or in milk. The coop is moved in two weeks, always to dry, clean quarters and away from any animal pests. If the weather is pleasant, when the turks are a month old turn the hen out. Three times a day is often enough to feed them now. Always be sure they are in their coop at night and do not let them out until the dew is off, or if it is stormy. The turkey hen will only go a short distance when turks are young, and will stop wherever a storm overtakes her and hover her young, while a common hen tries to see how much ground she can cover in a day, and runs for shelter when it rains. We have never lost a turkey from gapes or roup and never a small one from cholera.

After the turks are half grown, if they have good forage, feed twice a day, always being sure they are at home at night and counted. If the gobbler shows a bad disposition and kills young turks or chickens, dispose of him as soon as practicable. We have had hens lay a second time when turks were a month old, and the tom assumed the care of her first flock. Feed your turks for growth until Nov. 1, when those to be fattened should be separated from breeding stock, and feed plenty of corn and corn meal. The last week it is well to coop them up.

The best results in marketing turkeys are obtained by taking an order book and going to private houses and taking orders, noting size and sex wished, as some prefer a hen, some a tom. Do not try to sell your turkeys all in one week, if you have many. To kill turkeys, drive two posts in the ground ten feet apart, and have the posts about six feet high. On top nail a scantling. To the scantling, or pole, tie a tarred cord with a slip noose at lower end. Catch your turkey and slip its legs through the noose and let it hang head downward. Catch the head in your left hand and with a sharp knife in right hand, open the turkey's mouth and run the knife blade down the throat, cutting toward top of the head on both sides of the throat. Let hang until perfectly bled. This, done deftly and quickly, is the neatest and most humane method of killing. You can hang three or four up at once and they will not bruise themselves flopping about. Find out whether your market demands the head on or not.

Whether you pick dry or scald, plump them by dipping, after being picked, first in clear, scalding water, and then in cold. Wipe the inside carefully with a clean cloth. Cut as neat a vent as possible and pull the crop out through that, never cutting over the crop. Be sure the windpipe is removed, and for private families, who usually wish the head removed, bring the skin up over the top of the neck and tie neatly with white cord. The turkeys should have no feed the night before killing. Be sure to infuse new blood in your flock each year, either by changing toms or hens, or get a dozen eggs to raise your own "new blood." The secrets of turkey raising are, freedom from lice, clean, dry feed, and dry, clean quarters, and do not try to convert them to your habits, but try to conform to theirs.

THIRD PRIZE ESSAY.

BY MISS E. J. PINE, BERKSHIRE COUNTY, MASS.

My experience in raising turkeys has been a very successful one, extending over quite a number of years. I think the time when I first became the proud possessor of a turkey all my own, will never fade from my memory. A kind neighbor gave me a young hen turkey when I was quite a little girl, and from the time when her hired man appeared with it under his arm I have been a turkey raiser. Purchasing three more hens and a gobbler, I managed to raise quite a large flock the first year.

I breed from only fine, healthy stock, saving my best for that purpose, and do not breed from the same stock long. I change my gobbler preferably every year and select hens from my own stock, as they are less inclined to wander away than strangers. The hen dearly loves a secluded spot for the nest, so it is well to prepare a place where she can slyly make a nest and deposit her eggs unknown. It is turkey nature to nest on the ground, and the eggs hatch better if exposed to the earth's moisture. I often place old barrels on their sides or set coops half around, and throw branches and twigs over them, and place hay and leaves carelessly inside for them to lay on in winter. When they come to sit, the nest is put in shape so there is no danger of the eggs becoming chilled. If, as sometimes occurs, the hen does not take the nests prepared, but seeks a nest in the wood near by, I follow and gather the eggs as laid. When she sits, I put shelter over her that can be closed up at night and opened every morning, to keep the wild "varmints" from her, and let her sit, providing she has chosen a reasonable place for the purpose. If moving is attempted, they are very "set," and will sometimes abandon a nest if moved, or so neglect the eggs, if shut in, that they fail to hatch. Sometimes there are one or two very early layers in the flock, too early to really care to set them, for early turkeys are not desirable, as the early rains and dampness are destructive. In this case I break these hens up and let them lay again, putting the surplus eggs under chicken hens. When I come to set them I prefer not to make mothers of the latter, as their habit is so different the little ones will not thrive with them after they begin to need a wider range. The lice of hens accumulate quickly and prove more fatal than their own and harder to get rid of, so I put little ones hatched by hens with turkey mothers.

Sometimes the wings of little turkeys grow faster than their bodies, and the quills stick out longer than the tail feathers; at the same time many dwindle, get thin and die. Unless the one in charge understands these symptoms, the loss may be great without the cause being suspected. Catch the little ones and carefully turn back the feathers which cover the root of the quills on the wing, and in between the quills will usually be found lice, which are sapping the life away. The surest remedy for turkey lice is one part kerosene to three parts oil; any oil which runs freely and will not get gummy on the feathers, is good. Put it in a slender-necked machine-oil can and let a little out along the roots of the feathers of each wing affected. The kerosene needs the oil, as alone it blisters the tender flesh and causes unnecessary suffering. Night is a good time to apply, just as they are put in the coop. Be careful not to get on too much, as that sticks the feathers down. Go over the flock a second time to make sure of a second crop; a large flock can be gone over very quickly.

After the patient mother has completed her time (from twenty-eight to thirty days), I teach her to come to the house every day for food, and then comes the time of caring for the little creatures, which are to be tended and kept growing into lordly young gobblers and meek plump hens to grace some festal board later on. I keep my eye on a hen which I know to be hatching, but never allow her to be disturbed to remove the little ones. If kept quiet, she will seldom kill any and will call them out of the nest herself.

The mother needs a refreshing dust bath often, as she has not left the nest while hatching. She is not confined, but the little ones are at first, while unsteady on their legs. I make a triangle of boards nailed together, which need not be very high nor very large, yet large enough for the mother to get in with her brood when she chooses. The little ones doze and enjoy the sun, while the hen dusts herself and picks grass and gravel at pleasure. The cheapest and most healthful food for little turkeys is curd made like cottage cheese, unseasoned. They are very fond of it and thrive upon it, with the insects of all kinds which they get. Stale bread soaked in sweet skimmed milk is for newly hatched poults. Milk is good for turkeys of all ages, but for young ones do not let it stand and get warm and sour. It is unnecessary to make egg bread, custard, cakes and expensive foods, they are rich, produce diarrhœa and must be guarded against. Make the food sweet and wholesome, as variety is not necessary, but do not give grease or meat of any kind.

In wheat localities, whole wheat boiled to bursting makes the best food, both for young turkeys and for fattening. Don't fuss with a healthy flock, but if there is a tendency to diarrhœa, pepper, black or red, mixed in the food, is a good remedy. As a tonic, give a small lump of copperas in the drinking water occasionally. Many lose small turkeys by keeping them too closely confined. Turkeys must have a range, in order to become strong and thrive. I have large coops for each mother, but unless necessary they are not shut up after the dew is off the grass, excepting rainy days. They run in an orchard, and the little bodies grow broad and the legs get the stocky look of thrifty little turkeys; when a little older they stay very contentedly in my meadow nearly all day.

THE CARE OF THE COOPS.—A turkey hates to get into her coop at night unless it has been moved during the day. If it is changed every day she soon regards it as a safe place to keep her little family over night. Should it rain in the night, change it that it may be clean for the day. Filth is a deadly foe to a young turkey in confinement. I have always kept my coops on the ground. An experienced raiser who has tried floors prefers the ground, as it is more natural and healthful. I think it is a good plan to keep a box skunk trap set at night near the coops.

When the turkeys get large enough to fly over a stone wall, they will wander farther away, and there is danger from hawks and foxes. I keep track of their whereabouts as well as I can, which takes me out doors no more than is necessary for my good health. I have had them so wild that they have caused me considerable trouble, but it was caused by introducing new blood through strange hens instead of the gobbler. The latter is the better way.

THE TURKEY DIET.—The curd diet is excellent while it lasts, but much is required as they grow larger. While they are small a little goes a great way, even feeding five times a day. I prefer whole buckwheat to any food, when my supply of curd runs short. It is healthful and prevents diarrhœa. The finest turkeys I ever raised were fed almost exclusively on fresh curd and buckwheat. Cracked corn, wheat and buckwheat is good food when they have grown large.

As soon as they show a desire to roost, I encourage them, providing it gives promise of fair weather in which to make the new departure. I accordingly introduce them to the turkey tree, a large maple tree in which generations of turkeys have roosted before them, providing a narrow board with cleats to climb upon. They are soon up and off in the morning without waiting for breakfast, preferring grasshoppers and crickets to anything I might offer, returning often about 10 or 11 a. m. to rest and refresh themselves with cool buttermilk, sweet skim milk or whatever I have for them. I make it a point to offer them something to encourage them to come home.

A turkey regards home as a place to get something to eat. It is well always to feed when shutting them up at night, which should be at 5 p. m. when small, as after that time they get so sleepy it is slow work. This teaches them to expect supper, and they will soon come of their own accord. When large, the supper need not be a very hearty one, as they don't need it if there are plenty of bugs, but just for the principle of the thing, to get them home, it is best to offer a reward. When feeding buckwheat for the first time, they rush around in a confiding way they have, expecting the familiar food of curd. Seeing only buckwheat, a universal cry of "quit" will be set up all along the line, and it is only after careful examination and thoughtful observation of the fact that the mothers are eating, that they can be induced to touch the stuff of which they are afterwards always so fond. After the flock goes to roost they are usually very little trouble until marketing.

I suffer very little loss from sickness, but hawks and foxes sometimes make sad havoc. I fatten on whole corn, with an occasional feed of buckwheat to counteract bowel looseness. Clear Indian meal is a harmful food at any time for turkeys, but mixed with boiled potatoes it makes an appetizing change and does not have the bad effect of the clear meal.

They should be provided with gravel to assist the digestive process, and have pure water within reach. Some shut them up; I do not. Norfolk, the great English county for fine turkeys, fattens them by filling a trough with corn and good barley. Besides that, two meals a day of as much barley meal as they will eat, with gravel, etc., is given.

WELL-DRESSED FOWLS PAY BEST.—The following rules may be observed with profit: Do not feed the fowls the morning they are to be killed. Full crops look bad and are liable to sour if left in. Bleeding in the neck produces finer-flavored and whiter meat than when killed in any other way. Some markets demand scalded birds, and others dry picked. As I dispose of my turkeys to customers,

I dry pick them, as they command a better price than scalded ones. Pick quickly, while the bird is bleeding and the body is yet warm, being careful not to tear the tender skin; remove all pin feathers and cut the wings off neatly. Draw, without making a larger incision than necessary, and tie the wings so they will lie snugly at the sides when cold, leaving the head on until morning, as the neck then presents a much better appearance. Many things I have mentioned as necessary may seem burdensome to the beginner, but after raising a healthy flock or two, these little acts insuring success will be easy to remember, especially as each flock is so like its predecessor as to be indistinguishable from it in looks, actions and the care required.

KENTUCKY METHODS.

ELIZABETH KNOX TARKINGTON, BOYLE COUNTY.

When the turkeys are matured, select the largest and finest for breeding purposes. This may be done as early as Thanksgiving, or as late as the first of January. For instance, in the Bronze variety, select by weight, choosing those of uniform bronze color, noting also the color of the legs, which should be red. Select young toms weighing not less than twenty pounds. The tom increases greatly in weight after the first eight months, frequently weighing thirty-five or forty pounds when in the second year. If the birds are poor and of light weight, a tom may be selected by the size and length of his legs. A large foot and long leg indicate that the bird will one day be large, if sufficient food and range are allowed him. From five to eight hens are sufficient for the average farm.

I would enjoin the person who undertakes to raise turkeys to keep them tame. This can easily be done by feeding. The turkey is a voracious fowl, and the grown turkey can never, apparently, get too much to eat. When perfectly familiarized, they are not apt to wander far in search of nests, which ought to be provided for them by turning a barrel upon the side, setting it in some out-of-the-way corner, and covering it with brush. The turkey loves to think that her nest is hidden from the eye of man. If the nest is provided with an egg, so much the better. In this barrel the turkey should be allowed to sit upon twenty eggs. Secure a large board in front of the barrel, which may be taken away for a short time each day, allowing the turkey to come off and feed. Care should be taken that the turkey returns; drive her to the nest if she stays off too long. A turkey may be moved to a barrel nest if treated after the above manner. After a week or two I find that they are as well pleased with their new quarters, and sit as well as if they had originally selected the spot. After eighteen years of turkey raising, I would not be willing to trust eggs to the nest unless I could secure the turkey upon it for the first week or two. After this time they become quite tame, and can be lifted off for food, which should be at hand. They will almost always return immediately.

When the eggs begin to hatch, take the young turkeys off and cover in a warm basket. The hen often crushes the young at this time if they are not removed. Fifty or sixty turkeys may be placed with two hens; they will not part company, and are not so apt to stray. It is natural for the turkey to wander away when she nests or rears her young. I pluck the long feathers from a wing of each mother; this renders them unable to fly over a tall fence. Young turkeys should be fed five or six times a day. Care should be taken to give only what the young turkeys can pick up. The best feed is curd, made from milk. This prevents the bowel trouble which is so fatal to young turkeys. No grain should be fed for the first six weeks. A pint of milk, boiled and thickened with three or four eggs, is fine food for young turkeys. A little pepper may be added to the feed from time to time. Corn meal bread soaked in milk, sour milk and scraps from the table, are all excellent. The old turkeys, when removed from the nest, should be greased beneath the wings, to prevent lice.

In raising turkeys, avoid as much as possible penning the young turkeys. Make a slatted coop and let them run in and out at will. When older, allow them free range of the lawn. Insects, fresh air and exercise are necessary to the well being of the turkey. Feed throughout the summer, and the turkeys will remain docile. When able to go upon the roost, drive to the roosting pole, and after a few evenings they will come of their own accord. If hogs are fattened, the turkeys will help themselves to corn and become marketable by Thanksgiving.

TURKEY RAISING IN ILLINOIS.

MRS. G. H. WATSON, JO DAVIESS COUNTY.

> See the gobbler strutting,
> Like a princely dude;
> See his harem meekly
> Foraging for food.

I change gobblers every year. Keep Bronze turkeys, the purer the better, as they will outweigh others, and are as healthy as any, unless it be the wild kind, which are not easily obtained in these days. I keep old hens, from two to five years old, if practicable, as they are tamer, lay larger eggs, and are better mothers and not so easily injured. It is not well to keep too heavy males. Never keep over a gobbler that is such a numskull that he will tramp the poults into the ground and then try to eat them. Such an one will kill more young turkeys and chickens than his head is worth. Every farm should have at least three (four to six is better) turkey hens and a gobbler. Although great eaters, they are also great foragers, and the annual crop of grasshoppers and other bugs ought to be utilized. After the young are a few weeks old, they need but little, if any, feeding, except in winter, or maybe a few weeks before marketing.

Early in the spring, before the turkey hens begin to lay, I put plenty of clean straw in boxes and barrels and hidden corners in and about the henhouse and yard; also at some distance from same under clumps of bushes, or any place that Mrs. Turkey will be apt to judge sufficiently secluded and cosy for her purpose, and my hens are not apt to stray to a great distance to nest. I put the first hatchings under common hens, as soon as I can get one to sit, as turkey hens will lay two or three hatchings of eggs if not allowed to sit; but I seldom try their tempers by taking more than one nest of eggs from each hen. When the common hens have hatched their young turkeys and they are ready to leave the nest, I grease with lard each hen under the wings and inside of thigh, to kill the lice, or they will devour the young turkeys. Then place them in dry, warm, roomy coops, with yard in front, at a distance from the other chickens, but do not keep them shut up an hour longer than necessary, as by running at large they will follow the hens better in a few days and will thrive much better, except in cold stormy weather. Turkeys belong to the runners, and must run or die. Better not feed them at all than to keep them shut up; hundreds of young turkeys are destroyed every year by confinement and improper feeding.

At first, I feed my young turkeys soaked bread, squeezed as dry as possible, and hard-boiled eggs mixed together, with a little pepper or ginger in it, and curds. Then, as they grow older, add corn bread, corn meal, wheat or wheat screenings, scraps of meat, boiled potatoes, and if they are confined, cabbage, chopped onions, etc., are essential, and plenty of clean water, and milk if I have it. If they are healthy and have a good range, they soon need but little care. If your little turkeys' wings seem to outgrow their bodies, they are not healthy.

Look out for the cause, which is generally lice and too narrow range.

Do not give young turkeys to common hens that are too heavy, if you can get a light one. The Brown and Buff Cochins are so lazy, lousy and heavy, that a young turkey has a poor chance of his life with one of them, and if she once sets her big foot on him his fate is sealed; he may live for a time, but must die in the end. These very large hens are not only heavy, but awkward and stupid. The Brown Leghorn is the best mother, except, of course, the turkey hen, that I ever knew for young turkeys. She is light and active, a great ranger, forager, scratcher and fighter; will provide for and protect her chicks, and if she happens to put a foot on one of them, which she is not apt to do, he is up again as lively as ever. Any small- or medium-sized hen is a better turkey mother than a very large one, but a large hen that has all outdoors to turn around in will not be so apt to crush the breath out of her turkeys as if in coop or pen.

When the turkey hens have laid their second hatchings, I let at least one of them have twelve or fourteen eggs, never more than fourteen, and put fourteen to sixteen under a couple of common hens. When the poults are out I give them all to the turkey and one of the hens, greasing the mothers under the wings and inside of thighs. To the other hen I give hens' eggs, or shut her up. As soon as I have enough eggs I set the first turkey that is ready; if I only have a few, I give them to a common hen, if they are in danger of becoming too stale to hatch, and let the rest of the turkeys lay and go to sitting when they are ready.

I have raised a flock of forty-two young turkeys with a turkey hen and a hen (two common hens for a couple of weeks). I gave them a very large, dry coop to roost in, with a good-sized yard in front. After they were a few weeks old I could not get a chance to feed them more than once a day, at night, as I did not shut them close, after a time; and soon they had no feeding, except what they foraged for over field and pasture. They grew like weeds, and I lost but three out of the flock. The turkey hen takes the hen away from the house, and the hen brings the turkey and brood home at night; so they are kept strong and healthy by free ranging; and, roosting near the house, are not so much exposed to wild animals, while two mothers can watch and protect the brood better than one, and they get along splendidly. The turkey will fairly take the heads off the rest of the hens if they come about to help eat the feed; but she will not touch her nurse, the hen; but will circle about and chase the other hens away while her hen and young turks do the eating. She doesn't get time to eat much herself.

If you have a half-dozen or more turkey hens, it is still a good plan to use a few common hens as hatchers and mothers. Beware of lice always. No young turkey can thrive with them, but when the turkeys and chickens run together they will get them. Trees are the safest and best roosting places for turkeys, young and old; so I let my young ones take to the trees as soon as possible. Never try to raise young turkeys by hand, if you can avoid it; it is a hard job. Never hatch turkey eggs in an incubator if it can be helped, unless you have hens or turkey hens to put them under as soon as hatched.

One spring my turkeys began to lay very early, while the snow was still on the ground; the hens were also laying, but not one of them would even talk about sitting. I kept eighteen turkey eggs until I feared they would spoil, and then fired up my incubator (one of my own invention), and put the eighteen turkey eggs and some hens' eggs in it. Although the turkey eggs had been laid while the weather was so cold and kept so long, the whole eighteen, when the time was up, had live poults chipping away, but three died in the shell and I only had fifteen live ones left; but they were about the largest, liveliest little turks that I ever saw. It was so cold that I had to put them in a large box by the kitchen stove, together with about sixty chicks hatched with them. Well, you would better believe there was a peeping and squeaking in that kitchen in a couple of weeks, when all the young things wanted to get out and run. At last, the weather moderating, I put them in the woodshed; the young turkeys all took cold and had sore throats. I treated them with sulphur and saved the most of them, but they were puny for a long time. If I had kept them warm till warm weather they would have done better; but when warm weather came, they hung about the door and I could not get rid of them. They seemed to think they must be where I was, as I was the only mother they knew. A cat got some, some died, and I only raised nine of them. I kept four of them for years, for mothers, and they were the best I ever knew, but it is a hard way (by hand) to raise turkeys, and I prefer almost any other.

If a turkey hen makes her nest by a field or pasture fence, away from the house, or in any exposed place where hogs or crows can reach it, make a low fence to keep out the hogs, and cover the nest with brush or boards to hide the eggs from the crows; but don't change the appearance of things so much as to scare away the turkey; but if she is an old hen used to being handled, she will not be easily disturbed. When my turkey hens go to sitting in an undesirable locality, I make a large, close, roomy nest with a small covered yard in front of it, and at night convey to it eggs and hen. I then shut her up close and keep her there for a couple of days and nights, then let her into the covered yard, where I feed and water her, then drive her back onto the nest if necessary (which is not often the case), and shut her in again. She will soon come out and eat and then go back on the eggs, and before the time is up you can leave open both nest and yard and let her go and come as she likes.

Crows are a great pest. They will steal the eggs, and are worse to catch the young turkeys than hawks, even, as there is seldom less than two, and often more, together, and while the old turkey is chasing one, another will pick up a young one and skip. She has to be lively and alert if she saves four or five out of a dozen, if they once begin on a brood, unless she changes her range, which she often does. Turkey raising is like all other employments. If you feel an interest in your work and attend strictly to business, you will soon have plenty of experience, and will succeed; but if you let the business take care of itself, you will fail.

THE NEW JERSEY SYSTEM.

MRS. S. WILLIAMS, UNION COUNTY.

Why have we such difficulty in raising birds naturally so hardy? Simply because in the domestic state they have deteriorated. The laws of natural selection and survival of the fittest, have been overlooked. In the wild state the weak, delicate turkeys die young; only the healthy live. When grown, the stronger turkeys kill and drive away the weaker, so that only strong, vigorous birds breed. Here lies the secret of success! Follow nature.

Do not sell your finest turkeys at Thanksgiving. Pick out your best hens, and as we must be even more precise than we have reason for believing nature to be, we should select hens two, or even three, years old; but the gobbler should not be more than one year old. He should be broad and heavy, and have thick, strong legs. From three to five hens may be allowed to one gobbler. Do not feed too fattening food in winter. Wheat, oats, milk and the privilege of picking young rye or wheat in the field, will put your stock in good form for the season. As to breed, I always liked the Narragansetts, as being a hardier breed than others.

Faults in the parentage show their result in the young in two or three weeks, or as soon as the wing feathers begin to grow nicely. The chicks do not seem bright as usual. Their wings droop, their steps are uncertain and tottering, and they stand sleeping in the sun much of the time. They grow very weak and die in two or three days, though, strictly speaking, they have been dying since their birth. There was not life enough in them to carry them through the feathering-out stage. No medicine on earth could have saved them, nor any care availed.

But suppose you have satisfactory parent birds, and have followed the rules for their keeping given above. Well, then, late in February, roll some barrels or boxes into out-of-the-way places, or stand a few sticks and boards tent fashion, among some shrubbery. A hen turkey likes to tread an intricate path to her nest, so it is well to pile up brush carelessly about these desirable nesting places. You should then throw a few leaves in each nest, or some old weedy hay, and you may put an egg in the nest or not, and then do not visit the place when the turkeys are in sight. Most hens begin to lay in March, although some lay in February, or perhaps not until April. If the egg is removed, the hen usually lays from eighteen to twenty-five eggs before hatching. If the eggs are unmolested, she will only lay as many as she can cover, which is about fifteen. If more are given, she will destroy them. Therefore it is best to set the extra eggs under fowl hens, and add them to the turkey's brood when both are hatched. A fowl hen makes an undesirable mother, as she frequents cowyards and the poultry runs, where young turkeys do not flourish. She also leaves them at too early an age.

When the turkey begins to hatch, go every morning, and throw her some corn or wheat, and see that she has water. She will thus become accustomed to you, and not exhaust your patience later, by hiding herself and brood from your gaze. When she has set twenty-eight days, the young turkeys are mostly out, but don't be impatient! About twenty-four hours after the first one is hatched, the hen will leave the nest. She does this early in the morning. You may throw in her accustomed food, but the little ones will eat nothing, in all probability. In the afternoon go again, with a boiled egg chopped fine, which the little turkeys will pick at in a lazy, wondering way. After this go twice each day, and always be sure to feed the mother with plenty of grain, as then she will not eat so much of the food you have been at so much trouble to prepare for the young, and having a full crop, she will not wander so far. Keep her from undesirable localities, but otherwise do not restrain her. After a few meals of boiled eggs, bread crumbs and curd, prepare a daily bill of fare, by baking a bread, made of one part corn meal, one part oat meal, two parts wheat shorts or middlings. Add a little salt and a little bone meal. Feed this dry in crumbs, except the crust, which should be soaked in milk. This dough must be mixed with either sweet or sour milk. Curd, or pot cheese, is always in order, and it should be seen to that the hen has, or can get, access to water.

Lice never trouble poultry that has a wide range. Roup is very dangerous to young turkeys. It usually comes in wet weather, and as prevention is better than cure, it is a good plan to drive the brood up on high ground over night, and give plenty of food, with a little pepper. If you could drive them under a shed or other shelter, it would be best, but this is not always possible. The only way, in such cases, is to feed so as to keep from wandering. If any chicks show signs of roup, separate from the flock, and put in a warm, dry place, and treat as you would a fowl chick with the roup. Diarrhœa is another fatal disease, and although a turkey hatched under proper conditions will usually escape both of these diseases, yet it is better to be on guard. Green corn usually causes the cholera or diarrhœa. Do not allow your turkeys to have it. If one falls sick with diarrhœa symptoms, separate from the rest and give one teaspoonful of kerosene oil. Repeat the next day, if necessary. Give raw egg if the turkey refuses to eat, and give sweet boiled milk with a little flour and whiskey or brandy added, to drink. Turkeys must be kept dry when roup or diarrhœa appears. In giving pepper, always give cayenne or red pepper. It aids digestion, while black or white pepper retards it. Too many give medicine, when none is required. It should not take the place of food, or be given with it when the bird is well. Late in summer the turkey hen hatches the second brood. On this occasion she does not need near so much care, as the weather is favorable, and also there is plenty of natural food to be had for the picking. However, keep your eye on her and be ready for emergencies. You will save yourself trouble by feeding twice a day as before.

TURKEY CULTURE IN NEW BRUNSWICK.
BY W. P. POOLE, CHARLOTTE COUNTY.

The old saying that "Like begets like," holds true in the breeding of turkeys. If your hens are small, ill-formed, and poorly bred, and your gobbler like the one Job was said to have owned, "So poor that he had but one feather in his tail, and had to lean against the fence to gobble," if you expect to raise good, large, marketable birds from such stock, you are going to be sadly disappointed. As well expect to raise a Brahma from the egg of a bantam, or a Toulouse goose from a duck egg. My experience has been that in order to raise first-class, marketable birds of from ten to fifteen pounds dressed weight, I must have breeding birds of the very best stock I can obtain.

In selecting my hens, I aim to get heavily built, broad-shouldered, bright-eyed, healthy-looking females, with firm legs, that stand well apart, and the general characteristics of a strong bird. Mate them with a pure-bred "Bronze gobbler," a fine, large, well-formed, warlike-looking bird, with life and strength enough in him to make the rest of the occupants of the barnyard quake with fear whenever his lordly strut is heard. Having thus selected your breeding birds, you have made a good, fair start toward success.

The sooner you can start your hens laying in the spring, the larger will be your young birds in the fall. In order to do this, give your hens, for their morning feed, hot mashed potatoes, mixed with corn meal and middlings, about two parts middlings to one of corn meal; stir in some pepper and meat scraps and a little salt. Just a word of caution here: Don't overdo the thing and get your birds too fat. Three quarts of this mixture will be enough for ten birds. In the afternoon, give a feed of grain, either barley, wheat, or buckwheat, or a mixture of the three. Provide plenty of broken oyster or clam shells, and good, clean water. It will not be long after the first of April that some morning one, and then another, of your turkeys, will steal away to some secluded place, and there lay her egg. It is best to let her have her own way in the selection of the nest, but keep your eye on her and take the egg from the nest after the turkey leaves it, leaving a china or hen's egg in its place for a nest egg. Turn your eggs once every day until you have enough for a setting, which is from nine to eleven, for a hen, and from twelve to fifteen for a turkey.

I always set my early ones under hens, as you can keep the young birds confined better when the weather is cold and wet. If you intend using a hen, select a good, quiet bird, one that will attend faithfully to business; let her set a few days, until she gets settled down to work, before giving her the eggs. See that she is free from lice, and that the nest is dry and warm and also free from vermin. Watch the hen and eggs closely during the period of incubation, and see that the hen has plenty of food and water within reach, so that she will not stay off the eggs too long. It is a good plan to take the hen off the nest every morning, and she will then usually go back to the nest immediately after eating. In about four weeks, the young turkeys will begin to break the shells, eager to enter upon life. Do not disturb them at this time, except to take the shells out of the nest, and do that as quietly as possible.

Let the little fellows stay in the nest undisturbed for at least thirty hours after hatching, then place them in a nice, dry, roomy coop in a sunny location. Place before them some fine chopped, hard-boiled egg, or a little bread soaked in milk, or both, and a shallow dish of pure water. Melt a tablespoonful of butter, add to this a few drops of kerosene; mix well, then dip your finger in the mixture and touch the young turkey on top of the head and under each wing. This will keep away lice, and that means a good deal, if you want your birds to thrive. After the young turkeys get so they can eat nicely, make some curd for them from sour milk. This is made by putting the sour milk on the stove in a tin dish; when hot, the curd will separate from the whey; pour the whey off, and when the curd is sufficiently cool, crumble it up and feed to the turkeys every two hours. Mix a little soaked bread with it (either brown or white will do), and put a little pepper in it, about twice a day. When about a week old, mix some corn meal (bolted) with sour milk or buttermilk, to a stiff batter, put in a little salt and enough soda to make it light. Bake in the oven until done. Then, when you want to feed your turkeys, soak a little of the bread until it is quite soft, then mix it with equal parts of the curd, and it will do you good to see the little fellows stuff themselves. Keep plenty of milk, sweet or sour, and good fresh water before them constantly. Gather a lot of fresh chickweed, or if you cannot get that, tender bunches of clover will answer; cut it up fine and mix it in their milk. When the days are warm and fine, let them out for a run in the fields for grasshoppers, which they are greedily fond of, but be sure the dew is all off the grass before you turn them out, as a wetting is generally fatal to the tender birds.

At six weeks of age, when they begin to show the red on the head and neck, "shooting the red," as it is called, feed them a little cracked wheat. At this time, and for some weeks, in connection with their bread food, mix a little bone meal with their bread, and you will find that it will afford much assistance to the young birds and prevent leg weakness. As the birds get older, you can vary their food, giving some whole grain when three months old, and a variety of any good food; above all, give them free range at this age, but still avoid getting them wet, as much as possible, as it prevents growth.

You have clear sailing from this time until you feed them for the market, at Thanksgiving or Christmas. I do not confine my turkeys when I fatten them. I find they do better when at liberty, for they will be more contented than when imprisoned, and when well fed will not roam about any to speak of, and take on fat much faster than when shut up. Feed them all they can eat at this time, —a mash of corn meal and potatoes, or clear corn meal mixed with milk is good, and plenty of grain, barley, wheat, or peas, or all together. I prefer the mixture.

To prove the value of the course of treatment prescribed in this essay, I will just give a little of my experience with a small flock of turkeys. I set eleven turkey eggs under a common hen. They were from good stock, but not pure bred. The eggs all hatched, and from the very start they grew very fast, and not a bit of disease or lameness ever troubled those eleven turkeys; they were the most even-sized lot I ever saw, and were the admiration of all who saw them. At Christmas time, when they were taken to the block, they were just about as much as I could carry; they dressed from eleven to fifteen and one-half pounds each, and were as fat as butter. I sold five of them for $11.50. "Go thou and do likewise."

THE FAMOUS RHODE ISLAND SYSTEM.

Of late years Prudence Island has been one of the leading turkey-producing sections. Over 800 turkeys were raised there in 1892. George Tucker raises the largest number, and probably produces more turkeys than any one in Rhode Island. In 1888 he raised 225 turkeys from 22 hens; in 1889, 306 from 28 hens; in 1890, 340 from 30 hens; in 1891, 322 from 36 hens; in 1892, 425 from 35 hens, and this season, at this date, he has over 300 young turkeys on the way to maturity. Previous to 1888 he had only average success, but since that time, owing to an improvement in his management, he has had but very little loss. He credits his present success to having gained a clearer understanding of the requirements of turkeys, as well as to having procured from Connecticut a very fine gobbler, by means of which he increased the hardiness of his flock. He has since been more careful in selecting new blood.

He found that young turkeys that were kept near the house or under the trees in the orchard, did not thrive; many had swelled heads and soon died. On the other hand, those placed on the highest and dryest pastures, where there were no trees and but a light growth of grass, did the best of all. He usually winters from twenty to thirty-five hen turkeys and two gobblers. One gobbler is sufficient, but the second is kept in case one should die or fail in any way. The gobblers weigh from thirty to thirty-five pounds and usually are kept two seasons, and the hens two or three seasons, old hens being the surest breeders. They roost out in the trees the year through, and but few are lost. In the spring a sufficient number of nests are made for the hens by placing barrels by the walls and fences near the house and barns, or by laying wide boards against the walls. In them is placed leaves or cut straw. The turkeys readily take possession of these nests, although some persist in seeking out one of their own. This is usually allowed unless a swampy location, or one too far away, is chosen, when the nest is broken up and the hen induced to choose another.

Sometimes several lay in the same nest. To prevent this, a nest in which a turkey has commenced to lay is, after she has deposited her egg, shut up for the remainder of the day, to keep out intruders. When the crows eat eggs laid in the nests that are far from the house, they are frightened away by strings stretched across near the nest. Glass nest eggs are used. Eggs are gathered daily, to prevent their being chilled, and that rats may not get them. They are kept in pans, having a few oats in the bottom to prevent their rolling about. Each panful holds two sittings, and is dated, that their age may be known. When a hen stays on the nest for two nights, seventeen of the oldest eggs are given her; the eggs laid by her during the two days are not left in the nest. The nests are first shaped, so that they will not be so flat as to allow the eggs to roll out, or so deep as to cause them to be piled one upon another. The turkeys seem to do better if not fed while sitting. Those occupying nests near together are looked after daily, to see that they return to their own nests.

Mr. Tucker at first experienced some trouble in having turkeys come off with a few young, those late in hatching being left to their fate. This was partly overcome by setting eggs of the same age. By feeding hens with dough when the eggs are due to hatch, they are also contented to stay on the nest longer. When the turkeys are a couple of days old and seem quite strong, they are placed in a basket, and with the hen, removed to a remote part of the farm. Triangular pens, made of three boards, twelve feet long and one foot high, are placed in the fields, where it is intended the flocks shall stay until nearly grown. They are not located near together, lest the different flocks attract each other's attention. But four or five of the pens are put in a twenty-acre field. The little turkeys or poults are put in one of these pens with some dough, and the hen is gently placed beside them. In releasing the hen, Mr. Tucker takes pains to step quickly back toward the wind, that, if frightened, she may go in a direction in which the cries of her young may be heard. and bring her to them. The pens are removed to fresh ground frequently. Care is taken that the pens are placed on ground free from hollows that may hold water, for some turkeys, when hovering their brood in such places, will remain in them while they fill with rain and the brood is drowned. After five or six days, when the young are strong enough to follow the hen without being worn out, and have become so familiar with the attendant that they will come when called, they are let out of the pens and allowed free range.

In feeding and looking after this number of turkeys, the attendant, usually one of Mr. Tucker's daughters, has to walk about three miles to go the rounds. Until four weeks old their food consists of corn meal mixed with sour milk, and they are given sour milk to drink, no water being given them. When four weeks old, cracked corn is mixed with the meal, and the quantity is gradually increased, until at eight or ten weeks old their feed consists of cracked corn moistened with sour milk. Until June 1st they are fed three times each day. From June 1st to July 15th they are fed twice a day. After this Mr. Tucker used to give them no feed until they commenced to come to the house, in the latter part of September, when a little whole corn was given them daily, but of late years, he has thought they did not get enough without it and has continued the feed the whole season.

In November they are given all the corn they will eat. They like northern white flint corn the best, fatten most rapidly on it, and the quality of the flesh is also finer when it is given. If fed new corn, they have bowel trouble. Mr. Tucker usually gives old and new corn mixed, for fattening. When the young turkeys get to be the size of quails, two hens and their flocks usually join forces and roam together until fall. In the fall the sexes separate, the gobblers going together in one flock and the hens in another. About Thanksgiving, the litters hatched in the latter half of May weigh, gobblers eighteen to twenty pounds, and hens ten to eleven pounds each. Mr. Tucker does not care to raise second litters. When he has them, it is because the hens have stolen their nests. He has considerable loss among late turkeys, and if such birds are kept over winter they get sick more readily, and as disease spreads very quickly among turkeys, he looks upon them as disease breeders.

The turkeys of the early litters that are lost generally die during the first week, or in August, when two or three months old. There are no foxes, weasels or skunks on the island. Mr. Tucker prefers birds with short legs, as they have the plumpest bodies. His turkeys are a mixture. Many are of a light gray color, similar to Narragansett turkeys. There are also buff, brown and dark ones. He prefers the brown and gray to the black, as they look better when dressed. He finds medium weights sell best except at Thanksgiving, Christmas or New Year.

THE WISCONSIN IDEA.

MARY C. BARRETT, LAFAYETTE COUNTY.

Four years ago I commenced turkey raising in connection with my other poultry. I started with all the advice I could obtain from those who had had experience in that line. But I soon found there was nothing like actual experience of your own. After disposing of my surplus stock during the holidays, I accustom my turkey hens to the poultry house as much as possible, and try to make them roost there. After they commence laying, I usually have some trouble in finding their nest, but by confining them in the henhouse till about noon and then giving them their liberty, by following them, you can easily find their nest. I take all the turkey eggs from the nest, leaving a hen's egg or china nest egg. Gather the eggs every day. Never frighten your turkeys, but endeavor to have them as tame as possible, so you can handle them on the nests. If I wish them to lay a second laying, I set the first eggs under common hens, eight eggs to a hen.

After she has made up her mind to set, confine the turkey about three days, and she will soon start to laying her second clutch. If, when I am ready to set her, I do not consider her nest in a suitable place, I wait two or three days after she commences to stay on the nest at night. Then I fix a nest in some place where I can keep her shut up during the period of incubation; some old building, where she will have plenty of room to move around in. Keep feed and fresh water near her, so she can have it when she comes off her nest to eat. Place seventeen eggs in the nest, remove the hen from her nest, place her in the building, and she will finally settle down to business in the new place without much trouble. Never allow her any eggs in her own nest after she wants to set; if you do, she will not take kindly to the one you have provided for her. (If she has laid more than seventeen eggs, set the balance under a common hen, and give the young turks to the turkey hen when hatched.)

After confining the turkey hen, never allow her her liberty till she has hatched her eggs. If, on the other hand, she has a good nest of her own, I allow her to remain there, taking note of the time I set her, so I will know when to look for little turkeys, which will be twenty-eight days from the time you set her.

After the turkeys are all hatched, I take the mother and place her in a large, dry coop with floor, that has been previously provided. Take the little turkeys and dust each one with Persian insect powder; rub on the top of head, under the wings, and sprinkle on their backs. Take an old pan or basket, put paper in the bottom, put little turkeys in, and cover them over with old cloth or sack; let remain a half-hour and then give them to the turkey hen. You will find the dead lice in the bottom of pan. By treating them this way, the insect powder has more effect than letting the little turks run immediately after using it. Rub the mother with it, also, and use it occasionally during the first two months of the turkey's life. The powder can be obtained from any reliable seed merchant for twenty-five cents, postpaid.

The little turkeys will commence to eat in twenty-four hours after hatching. I feed mine on hard-boiled eggs chopped fine, or bread soaked in sweet skimmed milk, for a week or ten days, then I give them corn meal and curds. Scald sour milk, pour off the whey, and the curds will be wet enough to moisten the meal sufficiently; add a little ground black pepper. I feed the little ones five times a day, and the mother twice, giving her corn and oats, and keep plenty of fresh water for them to drink, also sweet skim milk if I have it. I keep the hen confined in the coop for two months, but allow the little turks their liberty at all times. After they are two months old, I allow the mother her liberty, and then I have no more trouble with them, only to feed them with the other poultry. I know that keeping the turkey hens shut up so long is contrary to all directions, but I do so nevertheless. The coop must be kept clean, and must be large. I use large dry-goods boxes; they cost about fifty cents apiece, and will last for years.

If you have boys that are handy, have them make you a runway for the hen, with lath, although I have never had mine fixed that way. I move the coop where the hen can reach the grass, sometimes pull it and feed it to her, and also furnish her with sand and gravel. Where you let the little turkeys run with the common hens, you can allow the hens their liberty on fine days, after they become accustomed to the coop, for they will return to the coop at night, but I have never been able to make the turkey hens do so. If they once get free, they will sneak away and stay till the turkeys are quite old, and generally lose most of them. I had one turkey hen, shut in a box as described, and she raised twenty-one nice turkeys, and that was in 1892, when it rained so much.

THE PENNSYLVANIA SYSTEM.

MRS. A. CLARKE, CRAWFORD COUNTY.

Having been in the turkey business for a long time, I find that the best results are secured by careful attention to the following points: First—I take care that the parent birds are not related, never keeping over male and females from the same flock.

Second—Experiments have proven that eggs laid by turkeys two or three years old produce stronger and larger turkeys than those of the yearlings.

Third—Instead of allowing the turkeys to steal their nests, and hatch their broods where and when they like, I prepare large nests in convenient out-of-the-way places, and I find that the turkeys usually take kindly to them, and seem to appreciate the favor. However, if one shows a disposition to pick out a place for herself, I manage, if possible, to give her an outfit, in the shape of an old box, with a freshly cut sod and a little straw in the bottom, and a few boards for shelter, and allow her to remain. Then, taking charge of the fresh-laid eggs, I keep them carefully, until I have enough to set two turkeys and two hens at the same time, or as near that as possible. In order to do this, I do not allow the turkeys to set until after the second laying. I then give all the young turkeys that are hatched to the two old mother turkeys; they, each having a large brood, and being so near of an age, can run together without injury. I have invariably found that where there are several broods of different ages, the older ones will trample and pick the smaller ones to death before they are half grown.

When the little turkeys begin to eat, I feed them hard-boiled eggs, chopped fine, for the first week, then I begin feeding wheat bread, crumbled, and mixed with the eggs, and it is very amusing to see them pick eagerly around for the bits of egg, leaving the bread crumbs until they are obliged to eat them. They greatly prefer a diet of egg alone, but soon grow accustomed to the change. When they are about four weeks old, I begin mixing whole wheat with the bread, and continue this, using less bread, until they will eat the clear wheat. This, I think, makes the best food for growing turkeys.

Besides this, as soon as they are a couple of weeks old, I give them broken earthen ware, pounded up into small bits. To those who may think this a queer article of diet, I will say that I learned its value by accident. Some broken dishes were thrown into the turkey yard, and I found the turkeys trying to swallow them. Every bit that was small enough to go down their throats (and it is astonishing how great their capacity is in that direction), soon disappeared, and they clamored for more. I supplied them freely with ground oyster shells, thinking that would be much better. But no, the fastidious creatures turned from them in disgust, and I went to pounding up all the broken dishes I could find. I never saw fowls so eager for anything as they are for those sharp, white fragments. Nowadays if a dish is broken by accident, scarcely a sigh is heard, as some one exclaims, "Oh, save that for the turkeys." Strange as it may seem, no signs of the liver trouble which so frequently affects growing turkeys and so often proves fatal, has appeared among the flocks that have been treated to a generous supply of pounded crockery. Does any one ask how often this should be fed? I usually give it to them twice a day; after feeding them the morning and evening rations of bread and wheat, I take a few pieces of earthen ware, and placing them on a large stone near the feeding place, I break them into small bits. As they fly off into the grass, it is funny to see the little turkeys scramble after them, squeaking with delight. At first I feared that the large pieces which they greedily swallowed would kill them, but soon found that it only made them healthy and lively.

In addition to this, I keep the young turkeys from roaming through the dewy grass, by confining them in a board pen till they are at least two weeks old; then when larger I furnish a plentiful supply of wood ashes for dust baths, which keeps them free from lice. By following the above methods, I have had the best success in turkey culture, and consider it a paying enterprise. One thing you will notice that I have carefully avoided, viz.: The feeding of wet, raw foods, such as corn meal or chop mixed up with milk or water, as it does not digest easily, although, for a change, I occasionally give them fresh milk curds, with a little black pepper; and always supply them with clean drinking water.

HOW THE FAMOUS WESTERN NEW YORK TURKEYS ARE GROWN.

BY SARAH FRIES, ONTARIO COUNTY.

[*Our contributor is 73 years old, and has been a successful turkey raiser for fifty years.*]

I keep two gobblers and five hens, which are saved the previous season. As soon as I can gather eight or nine eggs, I place them under a sitting hen. Every morning I visit every hen and allow her to eat all the corn she will from my hand. When the little ones are a few hours old I place them, with their mother, in a slatted coop at once, giving them water in a shallow vessel filled with small stones, so the little ones could only dip their bills in. This I place outside the coop, in reach of the mother. I then feed them with carefully curdled milk, and a little wheat bran mixed in. When two or three days old I grease their heads and necks, to destroy lice, for there is always lice on them after being hatched by a hen. As age increases, I increase the quantity of bran in the feed. Boiled potatoes mashed with good oats, and wheat bran thinned to a mush, may be fed several times daily, scattered on the clean grass. Drive them into a loft at night, when a few weeks old, and they will learn to roost there and be safe. My first brood of two hundred fine turkeys were raised many years ago, and sold for eighteen cents dressed. They averaged two dollars each, bringing me the snug sum of four hundred dollars.

ONTARIO METHODS IN TURKEY RAISING.

MRS. JOHNSON A. GREEN, LEEDS COUNTY.

I have raised turkeys for the last twenty years, with good success, having flocks of from forty to eighty birds each year. The first requisite is good birds. I prefer Bronze. I select the best young hens from my flock, and if I have any old ones that have proved good mothers, keep them. I keep five or six hens and a gobbler. I look around in the fall, and get a good one from improved breed if possible, never keeping one from the same flock as the hens. I keep them in a house by themselves during winter, feeding liberally with mixed grain, and give pure water to drink, warming it in the coldest weather. They do not require as warm a house as hens, but want light, and prefer a high roost. I let them out for a run every day, except in stormy weather. I think keeping them tame during winter, never allowing them to be frightened by children or dogs, saves trouble when laying time comes, which, with mine, is about the first of April.

I then give them free access to the barns, leaving nest eggs where I wish them to lay, and I seldom have them lay outside the buildings or roaming the field in search of a brush pile to hide their nest. They generally lay from eighteen to twenty eggs. Should two or more choose to lay in the same nest, before they begin to set, I make a new nest a few feet to one side, and put a nest egg in it. One turkey will soon find it and leave the other in peace. When ready to set, put sixteen to eighteen eggs under each, protect from draughts, and if weather is cold, feed on the nest; if warm, they will come off for feed as often as necessary.

When hatching, do not be in a hurry to take them out of the nest, but leave them at least twenty-four hours. Then if it is a warm, sunny day, put them out. If the old one is inclined to ramble too far, put her in a coop with slat front, allowing the little ones to run in and out. Feed the first two or three days on hard-boiled eggs and bread soaked in sweet milk, squeezing it quite dry (I never feed anything soft or sloppy). When weather is damp or cold I add a little black pepper, and onion tops are always relished by them. When three or four days old I drop the eggs and feed, instead, with the soaked bread, curd made of buttermilk with a little sweet milk added. Let it come to the boil, dip out the curd while scalding hot, and mix with a little shorts. This added to soaked bread makes a splendid ration for young turkeys. As they get older I drop the bread and feed curd and shorts alone, and when about four or five weeks old they require quite a lot of shorts. I use some of the whey as well as the curd, always pouring it on the shorts scalding hot. I never feed anything else, nor do I ever give that without being thoroughly scalded. Feed five or six times a day for the first few days, then four times; when three weeks old, three times is sufficient, and twice a day at four weeks; give all they will eat morning and evening. Keep pure water in a shallow dish convenient.

I never have sick turkeys and seldom lose one except from accident. I shut them up at night for safety, and do not let them out until the dew is off, or nearly so. If a cold, damp morning, I feed them in the stable. If a sudden shower comes up, put in the turkeys; they cannot stand wet for the first six or eight weeks. When they have attained that age they are very hardy, able to get their own living, provided they have the run of the farm, as mine have, and will do better roosting out of doors. When preparing for market do not shut up to fatten, but feed well on corn and buckwheat and let them run out.

LIST OF ILLUSTRATIONS.

Frontispiece—The American Wild turkey	
Fig 1—Trap for Wild turkeys	11
2—"Calling" Wild turkeys	13
3—The Prize Bronze turkey	20
4—"Pure Blooded" Black turkeys	23
5—Pure-bred White Holland turkeys	27
6—Buff turkey cock	29
7—Narragansett turkeys	32
8—Pair of domesticated Brush turkeys	35
9—Wild blood turkeys	37
10—Pure wild gobbler bred in confinement	39
11—Part wild blood Bronze turkey	41
12—White Holland turkeys	44
13—Mr Bloodgood's flock of White Holland turkeys	47
14—Missouri prize-winning Bronze	49
15—Pen to confine little turkeys until old enough to jump over; mother at liberty	65
16—Rhode Island turkey shingle	67
17—Western style of turkey shingle	67
18—Coop for brooding turkey, while the chicks are at liberty	69
19—Shed for sheltering little turkeys at night	70
20—Shed for sheltering little turkeys at night	70
21—From a photograph of Browning & Chappell's flock, Rhode Island	74
22—Turkeys packed for market	77
23—Open crate for shipping dressed turkeys in cool weather	80
24—Suggestions for marking turkeys by their feet	88
25—No more trouble from straying turkeys	94
26—The gapeworm	99
27—Windpipe of a fowl	100
28—Cæca	102
29—Diseased cæca	103
30—One side or wing of the cæcum cut open, showing its diseased state	104
31—One cæcum from Fig. 29, slit open to show thickened mucous membrane	105
32—The other cæcum from Fig. 29, cut crosswise to show thickening	105
33—Spotted liver, due to "blackhead"	106
34—Natural size of spots on liver	196
35—Tapeworm from a turkey	111

INDEX.

A

Afflicted chickens	102
After killing	76
Air-slaked lime	101
Appendage, fleshy	71
Assorting, in packing	77
Attentive mothers	61

B

Babcock, by	22
Barber, by	18
Barns, free access to	153
Barrel nest	130
Barrett, Mary C., by	146
Battles of males	11
Beak of Bronze	16
Beginners	74
Best breed	36
Billy, the	71
Black, the	22
Black Norfolk	22
Black varieties	30
Blackhead, contagious	105
"Bleed Out," half	76
Bleeding, by	76
Blue	31
Body, choice feathers	82
Bone mill or cutter	68
Boston market, for	77
Boston at Thanksgiving	80
Bowel trouble	45
Breakfast for	52
Breeds, classification of	15
Breeders, for	50
Breeding stock, care of	51
Broilers, for fancy profits	71
Bronze, the	16
Bronze crosses	40
Brush, the	34
Buckwheat, whole	127
Buff, the	28
Buying	119

C

Call of	10
Cankers	98
Care of coop	126
Care of young	116
Catching in the fall	74
Charcoal, pounded, for	73
Chicago market for	76
Chill	69
Choice body feathers	82
Cholera, cure	188
Christmas, selling after	81
Clarke, Mrs. A., by	149
Classification of breeds	15
Color	18
Coloring of Narragansett	33
Common turkeys	36
Confine, do not	142
Confining the little at night	70
Cooked food	68
Coop, care of	126
Coop, roomy	66
Corn, green	138
Corn bread	70
Correspondent, by a	26
Cortez	1
Crosses	39
Crows, danger from	136
Curd diet	127

D

Day, second of hatching	65
Delicate colors	29
Derivation of name	3
Diseases	90
Diarrhœa	96
Diet, the	127
Domesticated in Mexico	2
Dosing breeding turkeys	110
Dressing, cost of	76
Dressing, rules for	128
Dust, bath	126

E

Early shipments	79
Earthen ware, broken	150
Eastern growers, losses of	106
Eggs, hatch best	120
Eggs of wild	7

INDEX.

Eggs, to insure fertile	119	Housed	51
Eggs, when begin to hatch	130	How to keep at home	111
Etymology of	1		
Europe, into	1	**I**	
Experience with an albino gobbler	6	Incubation	55
		Infusing fresh blood from wild turkey	37
F		Isolated when sick	118
Fanciers' Review, from	97	**J**	
Fascination for raising	48	Jews, name by	3
Fasten, to	120	Judging the Bronze	18
Fat, in autumn and early winter	8	**K**	
Fattening and marketing	72	Kentucky methods	129
Faults in parentage	137	Kill, to	123
Favorites, the	36	Killing, after	76
Feathers of Bronze	17	Killing	76
Feathers of	82	Killed, when	11
Feathers, choice body	82	Killing of young hens for market	47
Feathers, dry picked	83		
Feathers, price of	84	Kousso	111
Feathers, to ship	83	Koussein	111
Feathering period	68		
Feed	52	**L**	
Feed, after first	121	Late hatched	53
Feet, marking	89	Lavender	31
Female, the	48	Laying	13
Fencing	113	Layers, early	124
Food cooked	68	Laying and hatching	54
Food, deprive of	76	Leg weakness	111
Food, fourth week after hatching	117	Liberty of	70
		Lice	26
Food, green	68	Lice, to find	125
For breeders	50	Lime, air-slaked	101
France, in	58	Little turkeys	68
Fries, Sarah, by	151	Liver, disease of	106
Frightened	75	Loss, from foxes and hawks	128
		Lotion	98
G		London, at	34
Gapes	98	**M**	
Gobbler, the	40		
Gobblers, change	131	Males, battle of	11
Grease, head and neck	152	Male fern	111
Green, Mrs. Johnson A., by	152	Male, head of	16
Green food	68	Maltese	31
Growing, a business	43	Market birds, good	33
Grown, after half	122	Marketing	72
		Marketing turkey feathers	81
H		Marking	85
Habits, not changed	5	Mated, when	120
Half bled out	76	Matured, when	129
Half-blood hens	38	Mating	36
Half-wild gobblers	40	Matrimony	10
Hard-boiled eggs for young	117	Meal, first	65
Hatching, day of	65	Meguin, by	104
Head of male	16	Mexico, domesticated in	2
Hindrances	90	Mexico, from	1
Honduras, the	15	Mexican, the	15
Hot feed	53	Mongrels	36

Mother, best	133	Purchasing birds	95
Mothers, attentive	61	Pyrethrum for lice	92

N

Narragansett, coloring of	33	Quarter wild crosses	38
Narragansett, the	31		
Natural food	52		

R

Nests, barrel	130	Raisers of	73
Nests of the Brush	34	Raising by women	45
Nest of wild	5	Raising, fascinations of	48
Nests in field or pasture	135	Raising in Illinois	131
Nests, roomy	135	Raising, why difficult	136
New Brunswick, culture in	139	Range	43
New Jersey system	136	Rare color of buff	28
Newport, near	79	Rations, extra	72
New York market	77	Rearing the chicks	64
North American, the	15	Relations to peacock	2
Northern corn	69	Restives, the	59
Not hard to raise	44	Rhode Island experiment station	39
		Rhode Island's famous system	143

O

Old hands	74		
Old turkeys	46	Rhode Island Pattern	67
Ontario methods	152	Rhode Island Red	30
Origin	1	Romans, brought by	3
Origin of Bronze	16	Roosts, on	13
Origin of Narragansett	31	Roost, to	127
Origin of White Holland	25	Roup	97
Ornamental	9	Run, out for a	152
		Rudd, W. H., Son & Co., write	179

P

Packing	77		

S

Painting by Audubon	8	Salmon, Dr., by	109
Parent birds, not related	149	Scalded feathers	83
Parentage, faults of	139	Scalded stock	77
Parent stock, selection of	46	Scrofula	98
Parent stock, to replenish	46	Secondary feathers	21
Penning, avoid	131	Second hatchings, after	133
Pennsylvania system	149	Second prize essay	118
Pepper in food	69	Secrets of raising	123
Pepper, use	96	Selected parent birds	115
Peter Enty, by	25	Sell, best time to	79
Philadelphia market	77	Selling after Christmas	81
Pick, to	129	Sitting, to prevent	55
Picking	76	Sewell, by	34
Pills	98	Sexon, Mrs. A. J., by	46
Pine, Miss E. J., by	123	Sheds	86
Plumage	32	Shelter	85
Poor, if	129	Shingling	66
Potatoes, cooked for	73	Shipping	77
Poultry trains	80	Shipping in cold weather	78
Pounded crockery	68	Shrinks in dressing	76
Powder, to	56	Sick, isolated when	118
Prescott, by	1	Sitting in undesirable locality	135
Prevention of diseases	93		
Price	30	Size of Narragansett	33
Prize essays	115	Skin of young fowl	25
Profit in marketing feathers	82	Slate turkey	31
Prudence Island	143		

INDEX.

Slate varieties	30
Smith, Dr., by	108
Soaked bread, feed	132
Standard weight of Buffs	30
Standard of excellence	42
Start, to make a	118
Stevenson, W. E., by	62
Stiles, Dr., by	109
Storm, in a	122
Stun, never	76
Successful experience	123
Sutton, Mrs. C. P., by	118
Sweet milk for young	117
Symmetry, to get	19

T

Tail feathers	21
Tansy	111
Tapeworms, prevalence of	108
Tarkington, E. K., by	129
Thanksgiving at Boston	80
Thanksgiving, before	72
Thanksgiving shipments	80
Thieves	90
Third prize essay	123
Throw the red	70
Training to sit at any time	58
Trap for	14
Triangular pens	145
Tucker, experience of	39
Turkey tree	127
Tuscawara Reda	30
Two broods to one mother	118

V

Vermin, free from	140

W

Walter, Dr. H. D., by	100
Wattle or snout	16
Weak poults	26
Weight of Bronze	16
Weight of White Holland	25
Weight of Narragansett	31
Well-dressed pay best	128
Western breeders	50
Western New York, how grown	151
West, shipments from	81
Western shippers	78
Western style of board	67
Wet, raw food, avoid	151
White Holland	24
Whole buckwheat	127
Wild state, in	54
Wild turkeys' eggs	38
Wild, where found	85
Williams, Mrs. S., by	136
Windbreak	5
Wings grow faster than bodies	125
Winter, training in	62
Wisconsin idea	146
Wolff, by	18
Wooing of	10
Worms	103

Y

Young, care of	116

SENT FREE ON APPLICATION

DESCRIPTIVE CATALOGUE

—OF—

RURAL BOOKS,

CONTAINING 116 8vo. PAGES,

PROFUSELY ILLUSTRATED, AND GIVING FULL DESCRIPTIONS OF NEARLY 600 WORKS ON THE FOLLOWING SUBJECTS:

Farm and Garden,
      Fruits, Flowers, Etc.
           Cattle, Sheep, and Swine,
Dogs, Horses, Riding, Etc.,
      Poultry, Pigeons, and Bees,
           Angling and Fishing,
Boating, Canoeing, and Sailing,
      Field Sports and Natural History,
           Hunting, Shooting, Etc.,
Architecture and Building,
      Landscape Gardening,
           Household and Miscellaneous

PUBLISHERS AND IMPORTERS:

ORANGE JUDD COMPANY,

52 & 54 Lafayette Place, New York.

Books will be Forwarded, postpaid, on receipt of Price.

STANDARD BOOKS.

Mushrooms: How to Grow Them.

Any one who has an ordinary house cellar, woodshed or barn, can grow Mushrooms. This is the most practical work on the subject ever written, and the only book on growing Mushrooms published in America. The author describes how he grows Mushrooms, and how they are grown for profit by the leading market gardeners, and for home use by the most successful private growers. Engravings drawn from nature expressly for this work. By Wm. Falconer. Cloth. Price, postpaid. 1.5.

Land Draining.

A Handbook for Farmers on the Principles and Practice of Draining, by Manly Miles, giving the results of his extended experience in laying tile drains. The directions for the laying out and the construction of tile drains will enable the farmer to avoid the errors of imperfect construction, and the disappointment that must necessarily follow. This manual for practical farmers will also be found convenient for references in regard to many questions that may arise in crop growing, aside from the special subjects of drainage of which it treats. Cloth, 12mo. 1.00

Allen's New American Farm Book.

The very best work on the subject; comprising all that can be condensed into an available volume. Originally by Richard L. Allen. Revised and greatly enlarged by Lewis F. Allen. Cloth, 12mo. 2.50

Henderson's Gardening for Profit.

By Peter Henderson. The standard work on Market and Family Gardening. The successful experience of the author for more than thirty years, and his willingness to tell, as he does in this work, the secret of his success for the benefit of others, enables him to give most valuable information. The book is profusely illustrated. Cloth, 12mo. 2.00

Henderson's Gardening for Pleasure.

A guide to the amateur in the fruit, vegetable and flower garden with full descriptions for the greenhouse, conservatory and window garden. It meets the wants of all classes in country, city and village who keep a garden for their own enjoyment rather than for the sale of products. By Peter Henderson. Finely Illustrated. Cloth, 12mo. 2.00

Johnson's How Crops Grow.

New Edition. A Treatise on the Chemical Composition, Structure and Life of the Plant. Revised Edition. This book is a guide to the knowledge of agricultural plants, their composition, their structure and modes of development and growth; of the complex organizations of plants, and the use of the parts; the germination of seeds, and the food of plants obtained both from the air and the soil. The book is a valuable one to all real students of agriculture. With numerous illustrations and tables of analysis. By Prof. Samuel W. Johnson of Yale College. Cloth, 12mo 2.00

Johnson's How Crops Feed.

A Treatise on the Atmosphere and the Soil, as related in the Nutrition of Agricultural Plants. This volume—the companion and complement to "How Crops Grow"—has been welcomed by those who appreciate the scientific aspects of agriculture. Illustrated. By Prof. Samuel W. Johnson. Cloth, 12mo. 2.00

Market Gardening and Farm Notes.

By Barnet Landreth. Experiences and Observations for both North and South, of interest to the Amateur Gardener, Trucker and Farmer. A novel feature of the book is the calendar of farm and garden operations for each month of the year; the chapters on fertilizers, transplanting, succession and rotation of crops, the packing, shipping and marketing of vegetables, will be especially useful to market gardeners. Cloth, 12mo. 1.00

Forest Planting.

A Treatise on the Care of Woodlands and the Restoration of the Denuded Timber-Lands on Plains and Mountains. By H. Nicholas Jarchow, LL. D. The author has fully described those European methods which have proved to be most useful in maintaining the superb forests of the old world. This experience has been adapted to the different climates and trees of America, full instructions being given for forest planting on our various kinds of soil and subsoil, whether on mountain or valley. Illustrated, 12mo. 1.50

Harris' Talks on Manures.

By Joseph Harris, M. S., author of "Walks and Talks on the Farm," "Harris on the Pig," etc. Revised and enlarged by the author. A series of familiar and practical talks between the author and the Deacon, the Doctor, and other neighbors, on the whole subject of manures and fertilizers; including a chapter especially written for it, by Sir John Bennet Lawes of Rothamsted, England. Cloth, 12mo. 1.75

Truck Farming at the South.

A work which gives the experience of a successful grower of vegetables or "truck" for Northern markets. Essential to any one who contemplates entering this promising field of Agriculture. By A. Oemler of Georgia. Illustrated, cloth, 12mo. 1.50

Sweet Potato Culture.

Giving full instructions from starting the plants to harvesting and storing the crop. With a chapter on the Chinese Yam. By James Fitz, Keswich, Va., author of "Southern Apple and Peach Culture." Cloth, 12mo. .60

Heinrich's Window Flower Garden.

The author is a practical florist, and this enterprising volume embodies his personal experiences in Window Gardening during a long period. New and enlarged edition. By Julius J. Heinrich. Fully illustrated. Cloth, 12mo. .75

Greenhouse Construction.

By Prof. L. R. Taft. A complete treatise on Greenhouse structures and arrangements of the various forms and styles of Plant Houses for professional florists as well as amateurs. All the best and most approved structures are so fully and clearly described that anyone who desires to build a Greenhouse will have no difficulty in determining the kind best suited to his purpose. The modern and most successful methods of heating and ventilating are fully treated upon. Special chapters are devoted to houses used for the growing of one kind of plants exclusively. The construction of hotbeds and frames receives appropriate attention. Over one hundred excellent illustrations, specially engraved for this work, make every point clear to the reader and add considerably to the artistic appearance of the book. Cloth, 12mo. 1.50

Bulbs and Tuberous-Rooted Plants.

By C. L. Allen. A complete treatise on the History, Description, Methods of Propagation and full Directions for the successful culture of Bulbs in the garden, Dwelling and Greenhouse. As generally treated, bulbs are an expensive luxury, while, when properly managed, they afford the greatest amount of pleasure at the least cost. The author of this book has for many years made bulb growing a specialty, and is a recognized authority on their cultivation and management. The illustrations which embellish this work have been drawn from nature, and have been engraved especially for this book. The cultural directions are plainly stated, practical and to the point. Cloth, 12mo. 2.00

Henderson's Practical Floriculture.

By Peter Henderson. A guide to the successful propagation and cultivation of florists' plants. The work is not one for florists and gardeners only, but the amateur's wants are constantly kept in mind, and we have a very complete treatise on the cultivation of flowers under glass, or in the open air, suited to those who grow flowers for pleasure as well as those who make them a matter of trade. Beautifully illustrated. New and enlarged edition. Cloth, 12mo. 1.50

Long's Ornamental Gardening for Americans.

A Treatise on Beautifying Homes, Rural Districts and Cemeteries. A plain and practical work at a moderate price, with numerous illustrations and instructions so plain that they may be readily followed. By Elias A. Long, Landscape Architect. Illustrated, Cloth, 12mo. 2.00

The Propagation of Plants.

By Andrew S. Fuller. Illustrated with numerous engravings. An eminently practical and useful work. Describing the process of hybridizing and crossing species and varieties, and also the many different modes by which cultivated plants may be propagated and multiplied. Cloth, 12mo. 1.50

Parsons on the Rose.

By Samuel B. Parsons. A treatise on the propagation, culture and history of the rose. New and revised edition. In his work upon the rose, Mr. Parsons has gathered up the curious legends concerning the flower, and gives us an idea of the esteem in which it was held in former times. A simple garden classification has been adopted, and the leading varieties under each class enumerated and briefly described. The chapters on multiplication, cultivation and training are very full, and the work is altogether one of the most complete before the public. Illustrated. Cloth, 12mo. 1.00

Henderson's Handbook of Plants.

This new edition comprises about fifty per cent. more genera than the former one, and embraces the botanical name, derivation, natural order, etc., together with a short history of the different genera, concise instructions for their propagation and culture, and all the leading local or common English names, together with a comprehensive glossary of Botanical and Technical terms. Plain instructions are also given for the cultivation of the principal vegetables, fruits and flowers. Cloth, large 8vo. 4.00

Barry's Fruit Garden.

By P. Barry. A standard work on Fruit and Fruit Trees; the author having had over thirty years' practical experience at the head of one of the largest nurseries in this country. New edition revised up to date. Invaluable to all fruit growers. Illustrated. Cloth, 12mo. 2.00

Fulton's Peach Culture.

This is the only practical guide to Peach Culture on the Delaware Peninsula, and is the best work upon the subject of peach growing for those who would be successful in that culture in any part of the country. It has been thoroughly revised and a large portion of it rewritten, by Hon. J. Alexander Fulton, the author, bringing it down to date. Cloth, 12mo. 1.50

Strawberry Culturist.

By Andrew S. Fuller. Containing the History, Sexuality, Field and Garden Culture of Strawberries, forcing or pot culture, how to grow from seed, hybridizing, and all information necessary to enable everybody to raise their own strawberries, together with a description of new varieties and a list of the best of the old sorts. Fully illustrated. Flexible cloth, 12mo. .25

Fuller's Small Fruit Culturist.

By Andrew S. Fuller. Rewritten, enlarged, and brought fully up to the present time. The book covers the whole ground of propagating Small Fruits, their culture, varieties, packing for market, etc. It is very finely and thoroughly illustrated, and makes an admirable companion to "The Grape Culturist," by the same well known author 1.50

STANDARD BOOKS.

Fuller's Grape Culturist.

By A. S. Fuller. This is one of the very best of works on the Culture of the Hardy Grapes, with full directions for all departments of propagation, culture, etc., with 150 excellent engravings, illustrating planting, training, grafting, etc. Cloth, 12mo. 1.50

Quinn's Pear Culture for Profit.

Teaching How to Raise Pears intelligently, and with the best results, how to find out the character of the soil, the best methods of preparing it, the best varieties to select under existing conditions, the best modes of planting, pruning, fertilizing, grafting, and utilizing the ground before the trees come into bearing, and finally of gathering and packing for market. Illustrated. By P. T. Quinn, practical horticulturist. Cloth, 12mo. 1.00

Husmann's American Grape Growing and Wine-Making.

By George Husmann of Talcoa vineyards, Napa, California. New and enlarged edition. With contributions from well know grape-growers, giving a wide range of experience. The author of this book is a recognized authority on the subject. Cloth, 12mo. 1.50

White's Cranberry Culture.

Contents:—Natural History.—History of Cultivation.—Choice of Location.—Preparing the Ground.—Planting the Vines.—Management of Meadows.—Flooding.—Enemies and Difficulties Overcome. —Picking.—Keeping.—Profit and Loss.—Letters from Practical Growers.—Insects Injurious to the Cranberry. By Joseph J. White, a practical grower. Illustrated. Cloth, 12mo. New and revised edition. 1.25

Fuller's Practical Forestry.

A Treatise on the Propagation, Planting and Cultivation, with a description and the botanical and proper names of all the indigenous trees of the United States, both Evergreen and Deciduous, with Notes on a large number of the most valuable Exotic Species. By Andrew S. Fuller, author of "Grape Culturist," "Small Fruit Culturist," etc. 1.50

Stewart's Irrigation for the Farm, Garden and Orchard.

This work is offered to those American Farmers and other cultivators of the soil who, from painful experience, can readily appreciate the losses which result from the scarcity of water at critical periods. By Henry Stewart. Fully illustrated. Cloth, 12mo. 1.50

Quinn's Money in the Garden.

By P. T. Quinn. The author gives in a plain, practical style, instructions on three distinct, although closely connected branches of gardening—the kitchen garden, market garden, and field culture, from successful practical experience for a term of years. Illustrated. Cloth, 12mo. 1.50

STANDARD BOOKS.

Roe's Play and Profit in My Garden.

By E. P. Roe. The author takes us to his garden on the rocky hillsides in the vicinity of West Point, and shows us how out of it, after four years' experience, he evoked a profit of $1,000, and this while carrying on pastoral and literary labor. It is very rarely that so much literary taste and skill are mated to so much agricultural experience and good sense. Cloth, 12mo. 1.50

The New Onion Culture.

By T. Greiner. This new work is written by one of our most successful agriculturists, and is full of new, original, and highly valuable matter of material interest to every one who raises onions in the family garden, or by the acre for market. By the process here described a crop of 2000 bushels per acre can be as easily raised as 500 or 600 bushels in the old way. Paper, 12mo. .50

The Dairyman's Manual.

By Henry Stewart, author of "The Shepherd's Manual," "Irrigation," etc. A useful and practical work, by a writer who is well known as thoroughly familiar with the subject of which he writes. Cloth, 12mo. 2.00

Allen's American Cattle.

Their History, Breeding and Management. By Lewis F. Allen. This book will be considered indispensable by every breeder of live stock. The large experience of the author in improving the character of American herds adds to the weight of his observations and has enabled him to produce a work which will at once make good his claims as a standard authority on the subject. New and revised edition. Illustrated. Cloth, 12mo. 2.50

Profits in Poultry.

Useful and ornamental Breeds and their Profitable Management. This excellent work contains the combined experience of a number of practical men in all departments of poultry raising. It is profusely illustrated and forms a unique and important addition to our poultry literature. Cloth, 12mo. 1.00

The American Standard of Perfection.

The recognized standard work on Poultry in this country, adopted by the American Poultry Association. It contains a complete description of all the recognized varieties of fowls, including turkeys, ducks and geese; gives instructions to judges; glossary of technical terms and nomenclature. It contains 244 pages, handsomely bound in cloth, embellished with title in gold on front cover. $1.00

Stoddard's An Egg Farm.

By H. H. Stoddard. The management of poultry in large numbers, being a series of articles written for the AMERICAN AGRICULTURIST. Illustrated. Cloth, 12mo. .50

Stewart's Shepherd's Manual.

A Valuable Practical Treatise on the Sheep for American farmers and sheep growers. It is so plain that a farmer or a farmer's son who has never kept a sheep, may learn from its pages how to manage a flock successfully, and yet so complete that even the experienced shepherd may gather many suggestions from it. The results of personal experience of some years with the characters of the various modern breeds of sheep, and the sheep raising capabilities of many portions of our extensive territory and that of Canada—and the careful study of the diseases to which our sheep are chiefly subject, with those by which they may eventually be afflicted through unforseen accidents—as well as the methods of management called for under our circumstances, are carefully described. By Henry Stewart. Illustrated. Cloth, 12mo.   1.50

Wright's Practical Poultry-Keeper.

By L. Wright. A complete and standard guide to the management of poultry, for domestic use, the markets or exhibition. It suits at once the plain poulterer, who must make the business pay, and the chicken fancier whose taste is for gay plumage and strange, bright birds. Illustrated. Cloth, 12mo. $2.00

Harris on the Pig.

New Edition. Revised and enlarged by the author. The points of the various English and American breeds are thoroughly discussed, and the great advantage of using thoroughbred males clearly shown. The work is equally valuable to the farmer who keeps but few pigs, and to the breeder on an extensive scale. By Joseph Harris. Illustrated. Cloth, 12mo.   1.50

The Farmer's Veterinary Adviser.

A guide to the Prevention and Treatment of Disease in Domestic Animals. This is one of the best works on this subject, and is especially designed to supply the need of the busy American Farmer, who can rarely avail himself of the advice of a Scientific Veterinarian. It is brought up to date and treats of the Prevention of Disease as well as of the Remedies. By Prof. Jas. Law. Cloth, Crown, 8vo.   3.00

Dadd's American Cattle Doctor.

By George H. Dadd, M. D., Veterinary Practitioner. To help every man to be his own cattle-doctor; giving the necessary information for preserving the health and curing the diseases of oxen, cows, sheep and swine, with a great variety of original recipes, and valuable information on farm and dairy management. Cloth, 12mo. 1.50

Cattle Breeding.

By Wm. Warfield. This work is by common consent the most valuable and pre-eminently practical treatise on cattle-breeding ever published in America, being the actual experience and observance of a practical man. Cloth, 12mo.   2.00

www.ingramcontent.com/pod-product-compliance
Lightning Source LLC
Chambersburg PA
CBHW020301170426
43202CB00008B/458